Stupid Things I Won't Do When I Get Old

Stupid Things
I Won't Do
When I Get Old

*A highly judgmental, unapologetically
honest accounting of all the things
our elders are doing wrong*

STEVEN PETROW
WITH ROSEANN FOLEY HENRY

CITADEL PRESS
Kensington Publishing Corp.
www.kensingtonbooks.com

CITADEL PRESS BOOKS are published by

Kensington Publishing Corp.
119 West 40th Street
New York, NY 10018

Copyright © 2021 Steven Petrow

All Kensington titles, imprints, and distributed lines are available at special quantity discounts for bulk purchases for sales promotions, premiums, fund-raising, educational, or institutional use.

Special book excerpts or customized printings can also be created to fit specific needs. For details, write or phone the office of the Kensington sales manager: Kensington Publishing Corp., 119 West 40th Street, New York, NY 10018, attn: Sales Department; phone 1-800-221-2647.

CITADEL PRESS and the Citadel logo are Reg. U.S. Pat. & TM Off.

ISBN-13: 978-0-8065-4100-6
ISBN-10: 0-8065-4100-8

First printing: July 2021

10 9 8 7 6 5 4 3 2

Printed in the United States of America

Library of Congress Cataloging-in-Publication Number: 2020945320

Electronic edition:

ISBN-13: 978-0-8065-4102-0 (e-book)
ISBN-10: 0-8065-4102-4 (e-book)

To the next generation in our family,
to my nieces and nephew—
Jessie and Caroline; Anna and William

And for my sister, Julie

It is not true that people stop pursuing dreams because they grow old, they grow old because they stop pursuing dreams.

—GABRIEL GARCÍA MÁRQUEZ

Contents

PART II: STUPID THINGS I WON'T DO TOMORROW – 107

PART III: STUPID THINGS I WON'T DO AT "THE END" – 199

Stupid Things I Won't Do When I Get Old

Introduction:
I Won't Become Like My
Parents When I Get Old

NOT LONG AFTER MY FIFTIETH BIRTHDAY (not coincidentally as my parents entered their sunset years), I began to keep a list of what I called "the stupid things I won't do when I get old." Truth be told, this tally—which kept getting longer and longer—proved to be a highly judgmental, not-quite-mean-spirited-but-close accounting of everything I thought my parents were doing wrong. My list covered all their poor choices, and I personally vowed not to blame the dog for my incontinence (Dad!), or to forgo a walker because it wrecked my outfit (Mom!), or to join the chorus of "organ recitals"—that litany of aches and pains, surgery and sciatica—at dinnertime (Mom *and* Dad!). Was I the son who knew best? Perhaps.

And as long as I'm confessing, my list even included shots at other "old" people I knew who were aging "wrongly" in my eyes. (Don't turn your house into a sauna. Don't climb up on the roof to clean the gutters. Stop driving before your license is revoked, or worse, someone gets hurt. Don't double-space after a period.)

I also knew that my parents (and others of their generation) were more than the sum of those aches, pains, and other sufferings. So much more.

Once my parents were gone, I reread the list with a new, and sometimes weepy, eye. I realized that this accounting of "stupid things" reflected my own frustration at watching them pay the price for being stubborn (a personal trait I know all too well). It also reflected my fear of what was to become of them as they shifted from "old" to "ill." I see more clearly now that I meant the list to serve as a pointed reminder—to *me*—to make different choices when I eventually crossed the threshold into my "senior," "sunset," or "silver" years. By writing these promises down, I hoped to ensure that I remember (and stick to) them. By sharing them in this book, I hope others may come to a greater awareness of the choices we make once we begin to think of ourselves as "old." I am often reminded of what my friend Andrew Weil, the nation's top integrative medicine physician, once wrote about aging: "We are not hostages to our fate."

At sixty-three, am I . . . old? It's certainly a question very much on my mind these days. It's also on the minds of a great many of the seventy million Baby Boomers, now that we're all fifty-five plus.

To get started on answering my question, I turned to friends on Facebook—my contemporaries—asking, "When does old begin?" Among the dozens of responses, two made me smile: "Old age is my current age + 4." And this one: "Tomorrow. Always tomorrow. Never today." I did smirk when a female friend wrote, "When you get called 'ma'am' instead of 'miss.'" (Men don't suffer that particular insult, although I die a little every time I'm called "sir" or asked, "What would the 'gentleman' like for dinner?")

Other friends pointed to new physical limitations as the line in the sand between midlife and old age. A work colleague posted, "When you can't jog a 15-minute mile anymore." "When I have to stop playing tennis," added my friend Thomas. I challenged these two, explaining that at forty I tore up my right knee and stopped both jogging and playing tennis. I wasn't old, but damn it, I sure was injured. (I took up tennis again fifteen years later—and have been playing an awful game ever since. But that's not my point! The point is that old is not synonymous with ill, disabled, or even injured.)

I also posed the question to some very smart researchers who've been hyper-focused on the definition of old. "Someone who is sixty years old today is middle-aged," explained Sergei Scherbov, who, along with Warren Sanderson, has pretty much redefined "old" for organizations like the United Nations and countries like the United States, Japan, and Senegal. Their research shows that the old age threshold in the United States is seventy-one for men and seventy-four for women.

Before I could pour myself a flute of champagne (or change my Tinder profile to say I'm "middle-aged"), Scherbov continued: "Our true age is not just the number of years we have lived." It depends on our personal characteristics—what we eat, how we exercise, whether we smoke, how happy we are (I'm sure we all know this list by heart)—basically, on our physical and mental health.

And don't forget that longer life expectancies and relatively low rates of disability and disease here in the U.S. also make a huge difference in extending middle age into our early seventies.

Former president Jimmy Carter tackled what it means to be old in his elegant book *The Virtues of Aging*. Carter—who is currently ninety-six, by the way—wrote, "The correct answer is that each of us is old when we think we are—when we accept an attitude of dormancy, dependence on others, a substantial limitation on our physical and mental activity.... This is not tied very closely to how many years we've lived." By that measure, no, I am not old, and you may not be either—even if you are a Boomer.

I think Lemmy Kilmister, the lead singer of the rock band Motörhead, nailed the answer when he declared, "I don't see why there should be a point where everyone decides you're too old. I'm not too old, and until I decide I'm too old I'll never be too f*cking old."

Age, like beauty, is in the eye of the beholder.

That's why two people of the same chronological age might answer the "am I old?" question so differently. Take this example: At a college reunion a few years ago, I listened to a talk by the silver-haired philanthropist David Rubenstein, who was then on the board of the Kennedy Center, the Smithsonian Institution, and the Council on Foreign Relations. *And* he held down a day job as co-executive chairman of the Carlyle Group, one of the world's largest and most successful private equity firms. In his talk to Duke alums, Rubenstein urged us to "accelerate" as we enter the last chapters of our lives. With his admonition in mind, I asked Rubenstein, then sixty-nine, if he considers himself old. "Sixty-nine seems like a teenager to me," he replied without missing a beat. Since then, he's divorced his wife, has continued to read a hundred books a year, and is a regular on the speaking circuit. No grass grows under this man's feet.

Just a few days earlier, Margaret (Peggy) Ingraham, a sixty-eight-year-old poet I know, in between surgeries to help mend a broken wrist, had told me sorrowfully, "I am an old lady now." Because of her injury, for the first time since she'd been a teen, Peggy could not drive her own car. She also needed to hire a home health aide, which further deepened her sense of dependence, creating a self-identity that was "old." "There were so many simple things I couldn't do, like open a jar or a bag of potato chips," she explained to me.

On the surface, it appears that physical independence, not age, made one of these near-septuagenarians feel like a teenager and the other like an old person. Indeed, loss of independence and mobility are among the core characteristics that define "old." But was her wrist the only thing bothering my poet friend? I don't believe so. She also told me that living alone led to her feeling socially isolated. (This was several years before the widespread isolation during the self-quarantines necessitated by the COVID-19 pandemic.)

Speaking of the pandemic, it's been hard for me not to miss the irony that anyone over sixty is now considered "old," according to the Centers for Disease Control and Prevention, and therefore at increased risk for severe illness, even death, from COVID-19. It's as though we've suddenly been required to wear a scarlet "O" for "old" around our necks, a kind of public humiliation and a refutation that old is a state of mind and not a number.

Attitude clearly plays a big part in this discussion. Once we start thinking of ourselves as old, it's so easy to fall into the trap of negative expectations. In fact, one study found that "priming older adults with negative attitudes toward aging results in immediate declines in psychological, physical and cognitive functions." I was actually astounded that a World Health Organization study reported that older adults subject to ageism lived on average 7.5 years less than people with positive views about getting older.

Granted, stereotypes of what it means to be old can be hard to avoid. Turn on the television, and you're likely to see (at least, if you watch the same programs I do): one of those commercials for the Clapper, the Life Alert medical bracelet ("I've fallen, and I can't get up!"), or that damn Jitterbug phone ("Bigger buttons, larger screens, and simpler menus"), not to mention the *Saturday Night Live* sketch showcasing the "Amazon Echo Silver" edition (designed for "the greatest generation," it will answer to any name even close to Alexa, like Allegra, Anita, and Alopecia, because, you know, old people can't remember things properly). We're shunned or caricatured—or both. We're even erased—we are nearly 50 percent of the U.S. population but only turn up in 15 percent of media images, from the movies to advertisements.

Looking back, I can see more readily how much of my own ageist judgment and shame colored how I saw my parents and the tone of my list. As my parents' health declined, my feelings often translated into a quickness to anger, a biting edge that now saddens me. My own fears of becoming old overrode my better judgment and my (usually) kinder self. But one other thing stood out: It is one thing to be "up in years," and it's another to allow yourself to be limited by your age.

Too often in my life, I've caved to the inner voice that's held me back. You may know that voice from your own head: "Not smart enough!"—"Fraud!"—"You don't deserve it!" I can't promise I will always follow my list to a T, or that I will never hear that voice again. But I can—and do—promise I won't give in to that voice when it cries "Too old!" When it does, I'll be sure to tell it: "Shut the f*ck up!"

And when it happens to you, I'll say, "Read my list!" Or start making your own. Today. And when the time comes, keep the promises you made to yourself.

PART I

Stupid Things I Won't Do Today

How old would you be if you didn't know how old you are?

—SATCHEL PAIGE

I Won't Color My Hair (Even If It Worked for Diane Sawyer)

The former ABC News anchor once gave me some smart direction when it comes to looking younger. I followed it for years—until an unfortunate adventure in hair coloring converted me into a silver fox.

FOR YEARS I'D BEEN A PATIENT of a noted dermatologist whom I knew to be twenty years my senior. He was pushing fifty when I first met him, and what I remember is this: "Dr. B" was very kind and skilled—zapping moles and lesions off my ears and back every year or so. He had a handsome, albeit craggy, face, and his hair was "unremarkable" (a nice blend of salt and pepper), which in medicalese is a good thing. Suddenly, after ten years, he appeared at my annual appointment with his hair dyed jet black. Whenever I saw him after that, I wondered who had given him such terrible advice. And really, where were his loved ones? Why had they not staged an intervention? Sadly, Dr. B did not look younger; he looked like someone desperately trying to appear younger.

I vowed to never let that happen to me.

Despite that lesson, believe me, I have worked hard to maintain my youthful vigor: I do yoga inversions, take ice baths, and drink Bulletproof coffee daily (replete with "brain octane fuel" to—allegedly—enhance cognition). And, of course, there's what my ex-husband referred to as my "persistent immaturity," which I prefer to think of as my *joie de vivre*. It has many forms: my neon-orange skinny jeans, boisterous outbursts, and a fanatical optimism about the future. I'm a devotee of Aldous Huxley, who wrote, "The secret of genius is to carry the spirit of the child into old age, which means never losing your enthusiasm."

I'm equally obsessive about my appearance: I slather on sunscreen, moisturize day and night, and choose only the most fashion-forward eyewear. If I'm going to be one hundred percent honest, a strategic nip and tuck around the eyes hasn't hurt, either. (Well, it actually did hurt, but the procedure successfully removed those weighty saddlebags.)

Despite the vow I took in my thirties ("I will never color my hair"), I have to admit I caved as I approached the mid-century mark. My hair, I now say with embarrassment, had become my armor, my shield—frankly, the most effective camouflage concealing my age. And I owe that strategy to Diane Sawyer.

"Steven and Diane" doesn't have quite the same ring to it as John Cougar Mellencamp's "Jack and Diane" ("two American kids growing up in the heartland"), but I was cohosting a benefit with the platinum-blond journalist (who once upon a time had won the Junior Miss pageant) when she gave me some unsolicited advice: "Anchors don't get older, they just get blonder." Actually, Sawyer—like me—started life as a brunette. But as one Hollywood hairstylist wrote in a blog post, "Diane Sawyer's big break came about when she changed her natural ash brown hair color to a glamorous honey blonde and the rest is history."

I'm skeptical that Sawyer's change of hair color transformed her from a beauty queen into an Emmy Award–winning journalist, but I did take her advice seriously. After all, even if there was just the tiniest of chances that a dye job had boosted her career, I figured it could only be good for mine, too. (Especially as my hair gradually became more salt than pepper.)

Make no mistake, I'm not the only guy looking to celebs for advice on hair color. One in five of men who color their hair admit they turn to actors, athletes, and social media influencers for inspiration. I'm guessing that they're more likely to look at Tom Cruise or Nicholas Cage than Diane Sawyer, but hey, she was the one next to me at the time.

I didn't just take Sawyer's advice to heart; I took it to my hairstylist, as well. For many years after that conversation, I visited a salon regularly for highlights. Every six weeks, my colorist added three separate blond tones— highlights and lowlights—to maintain my "true" color and to obscure the gradual infiltration of gray.

According to one research firm, I was hardly alone: 11 percent of Boomer men now color their hair to look younger, up from 3 percent in 1999. (My own hairstylist said about one in five of his fifty-plus male clients color their hair: "They are very secretive about doing this and don't want people to know. If you include guys who do it themselves at home, the percentage is likely even higher.") If I'm to believe the ads on my Facebook wall, we also color our beards, chest hair, and the hair "down there."

I knew this was a good career move: At the time, I was already the third oldest of the three hundred-some employees at an Internet start-up, and nearly twenty years older than my CEO boss. With younger folks replacing veterans, hair coloring seemed like just another way to stay at the top of my game. Or, more prosaically, to keep my job.

Still, I did not want to become my dermatologist; I did not want people talking behind my back about my fake-looking "dye job."

But then this happened: I had followed my honey-blond friend Molly to a new colorist (let's call him Alejandro), and one day I mentioned to him that I planned to tape a five-part video series later in the week to promote my new book. Alejandro offered me a "natural" coloring process that he enthusiastically promised would remove a third of my gray. "No one will notice," he promised. "And it's semipermanent," he added. In case I hated it, I could just wash it out.

Did I mention that the taping was in two days?

I said yes to the new process, and before I knew it, Alejandro had mixed together a thick paste that overwhelmed the salon with the scent of ammonia. He massaged it into my scalp, let it set, and thirty minutes later, he rinsed and dried it. Ta da! I had no gray hair whatsoever. But what I did have was ... unexpected, at best. I was a brash honey blond whose hair now screamed, "Dye job!" Alejandro told me I looked "fantastic," and one of his other clients desperately tried to help out, telling me, "Your hair matches your eyebrows now." Sure, if my eyebrows were the color of bananas.

I drove home trying hard to contain my despair and doing my best not to look in the rearview mirror. I couldn't bear to see what Alejandro had done to me. When I got home, my husband—a man who had never even noticed, much less commented on, a single haircut or color job in the many years we'd been together—could only stammer, "What did you *do*?"

"Semipermanent," I repeated to myself as I jumped in the shower. I shampooed a half-dozen times in a row, but alas, I could not wash the "honey" out of my hair. Nor the ammonia scent. My scalp, now more akin to a toxic Superfund site, stung from the processing chemicals. My normally fine hair felt brittle.

The next day, I got back into Alejandro's chair and endured a second chemical treatment to remove the color. It's no exaggeration to say that I almost suffocated from the toxic fumes this time. But it would be worth it to get rid of that awful color, right?

The results were even worse: My hair was now brassy on the sides and stark white on top!

With the upcoming video shoot that had inspired this ridiculous drama now T-minus twenty-four hours, I panicked. I put in a call to my friend Vicki, who serves as my personal Heloise. She recommended a Fifth Avenue "color correction specialist" (let's call her Bridgette), who squeezed me in at 8 a.m. the next morning, just hours before the video shoot.

I arrived with evidence, bringing Bridgette a handful of photos of my "real" hair color, which was really no such thing. She examined the damage with a series of long sighs. "This is nothing short of permanent," she explained, then proceeded to painstakingly hand color my hair, clusters of damaged strands at a time. Two hours later, she declared her "masterpiece" complete and sent me on my way—after I paid the $400 tab.

At the shoot later that day, nearly everyone commented on how good my hair looked, but I knew they were lying, because no one had ever mentioned my "unremarkable" hair color before. Finally, an honest friend came forward, accusing me of resembling a "trashy secretary from Staten Island." (I'm sure he meant no offense to anyone from the island borough, but I didn't take it as a compliment.)

I remembered what had gotten me into all this trouble—the Hollywood blogger who had written that "heads will turn and girlfriends will be green with envy when you show up with Diane Sawyer's style and hair color." Heads turned, it's true, but I don't think there was a speck of envy—or doubt about my dye job—in anyone's stares.

For the next three months, I counted down the days to the haircut that would permanently put an end to my life as a blond. It had become too much trouble to continue to be Diane Sawyer—and too costly.

I suspect I will always vacillate in my self-acceptance, especially as I age. But I've called a truce on my more superficial efforts, instead doubling down on downward dog and morning meditations, which are the real secrets behind my inner fountain of youth. These days, my hair is silver, naturally. I delight in all the YouTube "white hair bleach tutorial" videos instructing younger folks, those with brown and black hair, how to "DIY dark to platinum." All I have to say is this: Be careful what you wish for, friends.

I do, of course, continue to look to (male) celebrities for inspiration, and I can't help but notice all the men who are now silver foxes. Hugh Grant, Steve Carrell, Antonio Banderas—and of course, George Clooney and Richard Gere. To be fair, it's much easier for a guy to go gray. Diane Sawyer—like many women—is held to a completely different standard.

In the end, all this hair drama helped me to become more compassionate about my dermatologist's own error, because no one's hair should be the center of attention. Of course, I could have heeded the advice of a fortune cookie I cracked open years ago and saved myself a lot of trouble and money. "A man who dyes his hair badly looks desperate."

I Won't Double-Space After Periods

I know it gets harder to learn new things as you get older—but I will force myself to try. Not only that, I will shed the habits that mark me as geriatric, starting with the one I learned on a manual typewriter.

Nothing says you're old like putting two spaces after a period (or after an exclamation point, question mark, or anything else that ends a sentence). Yes, everything we learned in typing class is now passé.

For my thirteenth birthday, my grandmother, a typing teacher, gave me an Olympia SM known as "the Mercedes-Benz of typewriters." Every weekend, I went to her house for typing lessons, which always included multiple iterations of "the quick brown fox jumped over the lazy dog" (a sentence that contains all of the letters of the English alphabet, thereby working every finger from thumb to pinky). Before I'd repeat the sentence yet again,

Grandma often needed to remind me, "Two spaces after the period."

The rule became embedded in my DNA, as well as in the genes of everyone who learned to type before the PC revolution. Back in the typewriter age, all characters were created equal, at least in width. Fonts were mono-spaced, meaning that a slim "I" and a fat "M" were both given the same amount of horizontal space on the page. Sentences and paragraphs were thus rife with extra blank space around skinny letters. Without a second space after sentence-ending punctuation, it could be hard to see where the next sentence began. Thus the con-vention to put not one but two spaces between sentences. You're welcome.

Computers and word processors use what's called "proportionally spaced fonts," in which the spacing is ad-justed to the size of the letter, meaning there's no longer any need to double-space after a period. Turns out, that's an almost impossible habit for Boomers to unlearn—that little extra tap is embedded deep into our brains, where it's extremely tough to zap.

"I absolutely don't know I'm doing it," one friend told me. "I have tried for years to retrain myself, but I do it so automatically that I don't realize it until I see a printout of something I've written. The extra space stands out on paper like the parting of the Red Sea, but as I'm typing, my brain is connected to the keyboard through my hands without my fingers having anything to do with it at all." Fortunately for us laggards, Microsoft Word now flags double spaces as errors, ending the great space de-bate. Single-spacers, you take the victory.

Gen Y and Gen Zers never learned the two-space habit in the first place, which is why it has become the mark of our generation. As one (young) cultural critic put it, it's "totally, completely, utterly, and inarguably wrong" to put two spaces after a period. So we are going to have to retrain our brains—even my friend who swears she is absolutely incapable of stopping, and even you. Yes, you can.

Being able to change up an old habit is only half the battle. We don't just need to drop the outdated, we need to embrace—or at least learn—the new. These days, new almost always means technology. And fumbling with new devices, operating systems, and social media platforms is what truly marks us as Luddites.

Not convinced? Perhaps you remember that a few years ago, *Saturday Night Live* spoofed the Amazon Echo, better known as "Alexa," beginning with this cautionary sentence: "The latest technology isn't always easy for people of a certain age." Referring to a fictitious partnership between Amazon and AARP, the announcer declares that the "Amazon Echo Silver" edition is designed "specifically for the Greatest Generation." It is super loud and responds to any name remotely like Alexa, including Allegra, Odessa, Anita, Alberta, Alisha, Alessandra, Excedrin, and Alopecia. I especially liked the *SNL* promo for the Echo Silver's handy-dandy feature that helps old people find things.

> "Amelia, where did I put the phone?"
> "The phone is in your right hand."

Alexa also provides the latest in sports:

> "Clarissa, how many times did Satchel Paige
>   strike out last night?"
> "Satchel Paige died in 1982."
> "How many did he get?"
> "Satchel Paige died. Is dead."

Unlike other Alexa editions, this one also features an "'uh-huh' feature for long-rambling stories"—because you know the stereotype of old people, always repeating themselves.

Simultaneously hilarious and ageist, the skit highlighted several of the ways that our parents' generation struggles to master new devices, social media apps, and plain old email. Sure, we laugh—but it's not like we're doing so well right now, either.

For instance, one friend told me about her mother's struggles with the new TV she and her siblings had given her. "Mom loved the picture quality, but the remote just about did her in. We heard from neighbors that every so often, they'd get a call asking for help," she said. "We finally figured out that every time Mom accidentally hit 'menu,' she practically had to dial 911—she could press up and down on volume and channels, but the options on the menu were beyond her, so she'd need help getting back to a screen she recognized."

This friend got a good laugh about it at the time, but now she reports a newfound sympathy for her mom. "I have a Smart TV that's definitely smarter than I am," she told me. "I need two different remotes to operate the TV in the bedroom, and the kitchen set has a Roku on it that I don't understand at all. Don't even get me started on the two video game systems—only the teenagers in the house know how those work."

Personally, I actually worry about reaching a point when I just throw in the towel. My friend's mom, born before *radio* became common in homes, had to adapt to television, rotary telephones, record players (starting with the old 78s), push-button phones, answering machines, microwave ovens, and many more dizzying new inventions of the twentieth century. Can we blame her brain for saying "enough!" when it came to a twenty-first-century wireless remote? I think she gets a pass.

Certainly, there are plenty of people of our generation whose brains seem to be crying "enough!" these days. I'm not immune—maybe you do need to be a rocket scientist, after all. Right now, I have half a dozen chat windows open on my laptop as I plead for help getting several of my devices, apps, and programs to work. In one of those windows, the no-name Sonos rep keeps telling me, "You need to hardwire your speakers." ("I'm sorry," I explain, "I don't know what hard wiring is, which means I don't know how to do it.") Dashlane, my password manager app, refuses to provide a customer service phone number, so I'm looking at a laundry list of links to help me retrieve my "master password." (Damn. I didn't write it down because I thought the security app had my back.) Spotify—I love Spotify—won't stream again until the Sonos speakers work. But first, their customer service rep tells me, I have to download an updated version of iTunes. Before I'm allowed to do that, I must first upgrade my iPhone's operating system, but unfortunately iTunes doesn't recognize my phone, which means I can't download and install the latest version of macOS, then manually back up, restore, or sync these devices.

Finally, my "AppleBuddy," a thirtysomething tech wizard, made a house call. "That's ancient history," he tells me, referring to the lack of compatibility between the phone and operating system, although I feared it to be a judgment on me, too. "Just back up your device to the cloud," he says as he performs the entire operation in a minute flat.

At least I'm beyond some of the other day-to-day challenges faced by many people (some younger than I am!) who have hit the technology wall. Some are positively cringeworthy, including the dreaded "reply all" fiasco. I think almost all of us know how that goes: Someone lists everybody they know in the TO or CC line (thereby revealing all those email addresses to everyone else without permission). Before you know it, someone hits Reply All, and 716 people get a message saying "thanks!" That's followed by someone else asking to be removed from the conversation—a request also made to 716 people. Then people chime in to say, "Stop using Reply All!" (using Reply All, of course). If I can master using the BCC line, so can others. Let's stop the Reply All epidemic once and for all.

Then there's the more prosaic but no less vexing snafu, which seems epidemic among Boomers: the forwarded thread. If I never see another chain letter, scam warning, or subject line that reads, "Fwd: This is funny!" again, I'll be fine. What's doubly worse? Forwarding a conversation that may contain sensitive information down in the thread, without considering that the original sender didn't intend anyone else to see it.

"I forwarded an email chain to my boss—highlighting info about a project we were completing," a college friend confided. "Kind of forgot that the earlier emails in the chain consisted of me and a coworker complaining about how much of an idiot he is. Oops." (In addition to my "do not forward" advice, I'll add, "don't trash anyone in an email." It may end up in that person's inbox. But you knew that, right?)

Other instances of elder abuse of technology include using an AOL or Yahoo email address (listen, it's time to upgrade to Gmail or Outlook), posting deeply private messages on a friend's public Facebook wall ("Last night was great!"), or referring to Twitter as "The Twitter." While I'm on this rant, here are some other phrases to be avoided at all costs because of what they say about your age:

> "What's your fax number?" Sorry, it's past time to upgrade to a scanner.

> "Let's call a taxi!" Make that Uber or Lyft, and let your fingers do the talking on your keypad.

> "I left a message on your answering machine." What's that? Call it voicemail if you must, but really—just ditch any kind of voice messaging.

> "I printed the directions from MapQuest." Sweet. Now what will you do when the road

> ahead is closed? Most phones have real-time
> GPS in Google Maps—use it!

All of these scream OPOTLO (old person on the loose online!). Other marks of a neophyte include tagging photos without permission (especially if the friend you tag at the beach had called in sick) and leaving a voicemail instead of texting. You don't get "hipster" points if you use emojis and text abbreviations without understanding what they mean. (Hey, an eggplant is not just an eggplant, and "LOL" doesn't mean "lots of love.")

All of this is to say, I won't become a Luddite. *I won't become a Luddite.* I am determined to keep up, stay smart—at least as smart as my TV—and remain connected, even as that involves making new friends like Alexa, Allegra, and Odessa. Or whatever their names are.

On second thought, maybe I'm already a Luddite.

I Won't Be Afraid to Fall (Yes, You Read That Right)

I know I need a healthy fear of falling—at least enough to make me pay attention to where I'm walking. But I won't let that fear hold me back or make me hesitate.

I'VE ALWAYS BEEN AFRAID of falling. Maybe it's because I had two grandparents die as the result of falls. Then my dad died after years of tumbles, trips, and stumbles. But a few months after his death, I learned a surprising lesson about falling—on a surfboard in the Pacific, of all places.

During the surfing lesson, it's fair to say I spent most of the morning landing flat on my face or back. These weren't minor spills—I wiped out repeatedly, spectacularly, in front of my family and even a professional photographer (who hoped to make a buck or two from our surfboard adventures).

That lesson took place in the salty seas off Kailua-Kona on Hawaii's Big Island during a family vacation with my sister and brother, along with their spouses and kids. We had come there together to recover from a rough year, which had included the deaths of both of our parents, my sister's cancer diagnosis, my separation, and the placing of my brother's autistic son in a group home. Together, we were determined to celebrate our resiliency and newfound hope.

The first time I had tested my mettle on a Hawaiian longboard, I had been about half my current age, thirty-something and fearless—perfect attributes for catching oversized waves and experiencing long, exhilarating runs (as well as mash-ups with underwater coral and rough-hewn lava rocks). I loved the surge of adrenaline each run unleashed, fueling the desire to take on more and bigger waves.

Surfing at sixty was, frankly, much more of a challenge.

During those earlier surfing lessons, my muscles had an elasticity that made it almost effortless to "pop up" (that's when you move from lying prone on the board to crouching on it, butt out and back flat). Three decades later, I could see that elasticity in my twenty-one-year-old niece Jessie, a surfing novice, as she jumped up time and again to catch a wave. Her legs had a natural spring to them, and in a flash, she'd be in the Warrior II position, shimmying down the wave, braids flying out behind her.

I was not doing quite as well.

Sure, my hips and glutes have tightened over the decades, but the instructor, Ossian Farmer, pointed out that my body wasn't really the impediment. It was my attitude, my fear. "You keep hesitating, and that more than any loss of flexibility is holding you back," he told me.

That resonated with me. In my youth, I had had few hesitations. I was a Malcolm Gladwell *Blink* kind of guy: I could commit to a wave, a job, or a partner and never look back. Now on the board, no longer a youth, I found myself dragging one foot like an anchor caught on a rock. Turns out that in surfing, as in life, fear of falling can actually lead to more falls.

"The moment you hesitate in surfing is the moment you will find yourself in trouble," I read on SurferToday.com. You will lose momentum; you will miss the wave; you will likely wipe out. As Farmer put it to me: "Hesitation is totally the enemy. If you're not fully committed, you're history."

My niece Jessie agreed, saying it wasn't physical ability or even her youth that gave her an edge. "It's not a strength thing," she told me. "You have to be in your own body and have the intuition of knowing when to stand up." Having lived through so much of our family tumult, Jessie has had to learn a thing or two—at such a young age—about being able to stand up at the right time.

Surfing well, Farmer told me between my wipeouts, is a lot like meditation. "It's like not thinking," he said. "You're just in the moment." For the next several waves, I tried out a surfing mantra, similar to what I use to stay focused during meditation. "Eyes forward. Knees relaxed. Feet parallel. Core tight." But in the rush and flush of a wave, I got lost in all those words and wiped out.

I simplified my mantra to "Jessie," since her wave riding captured all those reminders. To my surprise, I caught the very next wave and made it halfway to shore. I had stopped thinking and was *actually* in the moment. As Jessie put it to me: "There's an element of risk each time you get up, because there's always a chance that you'll fall. But do you have the trust, the willingness to take the leap, when you don't know the specified conditions each time?"

Watching my niece, I noticed something else. Jess kept her eye on the prize, which on the board means looking straight ahead to the shore. I realized that even when I did pop up properly, my focus often wandered to the left or right, and I'd quickly tumble off the board. "Look straight ahead," my instructor shouted over the breaking surf. "Don't get sidetracked!" I couldn't help but think of the many times distraction had undermined me, personally and professionally, by tempting my focus away from the goal.

My siblings and I have lived through some difficult times and have gotten a bit too familiar with illness and disability, death, and fear. In the years since I'd last surfed, I had watched my aged parents fall and hurt themselves many times. They'd become terrified of falling, and yet they did, over and over. One afternoon, my mom tripped on a New York City curb, landing flat on her face. By the next morning, it looked as though someone had beaten her; her bruises drew from a Jackson Pollock palette—blue, purple, red, and blackish. "I don't remember what happened," she told me that afternoon.

With this incident and others in mind, I confessed to the instructor that I was afraid of falling. Farmer, who'd surfed since he was in third grade, admitted to some fears of his own, but he was philosophical about them. "Don't let fear get in the way of living your dreams. It will handicap you," he said. "Usually, fear holds you back and creates anxiety."

"But what do I do when I tumble?" I asked.

Learn how to fall, he advised. "Fall flat," he explained, which would keep me from getting scraped by any lava rocks. "Don't dive headfirst. And be as graceful as you can." I've now taken all this surfing advice as a metaphor for all future falls: Keep my focus. Check my fear. Learn how to fall. Watch my head. When I must go, go with the flow—and try to do it with some modicum of grace.

When it came time for the last wave that morning, I deployed all of my surfing mentor's advice, as well as my own experience. I popped up. I did a "Jessie" and caught the wave, surfing it all the way to the shore. Exhilarating. And then I fell—flat—since I actually didn't know any other way to get off the board.

My brother's wife, who witnessed this magnificent ride, had the last word after my head bobbed up from underneath the surf. After making sure that I wasn't hurt, she quipped: "The next step after falling is getting up again."

I Won't Stop Rocking Those "Too Young for You" Outfits

When I choose an "age-inappropriate" outfit, I will remember my mother's words—and her purple and Pucci wardrobe—and ignore those naysayers who caution me to dress my age.

"MOM, WHAT ARE YOU DOING?" I asked in mock horror when I walked into her bedroom. What she was doing was pretty innocuous—she was draped across the queen-sized bed, reading a novel—but what she was wearing? I could see a hint of purple silk undergarments under her stylish Miss Elaine nightgown. Well into her eighties, Mom looked downright glam, reminding me of what a friend says his mother once told him: "I may be a pathetic old lady, but I refuse to look like one."

I had long known that my mother—a plain Jane by day—was more of a Pucci and Gucci girl at night. Mom had always had a Cosmo girl sexuality that once struck me as "mother inappropriate," but she was extremely comfortable in her skin (no matter how much of it she revealed). She was defiant about fashion "truisms" and certainly didn't follow any that were age related. (Mom was never bound by sexist, ageist rules like no mini-skirts after forty or the prohibition on sleeveless tops after fifty.)

As we chatted that day, I glanced over to her dresser, where Mom displayed her wedding photograph from some sixty years earlier. Mom—let me use her very French first name, Margot—looked like no other 1950s bride I'd ever seen, except maybe the violet-eyed Elizabeth Taylor when she married Mike Todd in 1957. Mom had chosen a low-cut silk cocktail dress (what's known as a Shantung halter) with a flattering fit-and-flare trumpet skirt. It demanded that the wearer eschew a bra. The bride wore no jewelry except the simple engagement ring my father had given her (and which she later "upgraded") and her Cartier Tank watch. Not even earrings! I think those bare earlobes expressed her supreme sense of self-confidence. Mom's mother, an Upper West Side matron, had begged her to choose a more conventional wedding gown, but she refused. (To add insult to injury, Mom also refused to ask her sister to be maid of honor, but that's another story. She always did know how to buck tradition—and irritate those nearest and dearest.)

"What are you smiling at?" she queried, correctly reading my thoughts about her nighttime attire. Only recently, I'd been the target of my husband's ire over my own "age-inappropriate" attire. He did not approve of my neon-orange skinny jeans. He told me that the cropped navy velvet blazer I loved from Billy Reid was "too young" for me (even though the Billy Reid salesperson, a former Miss United States, declared, "it fits you perfectly"). I thought those choices preferable to wearing a sports coat with oversized lapels and power shoulder pads, not to mention the pleated khakis that seemed to be the uniform among my peers—all relics from the 1980s and '90s.

"I was just thinking how much we're alike," I replied to Mom's question.

My sartorial sensibility had not always been so, er, exuberant. Starting in my early twenties, I'd been very much a Brooks Brothers man; I even had my own go-to salesman, Lars, at the Madison Avenue flagship store. Lars kept me "preppy," dressed in 100 percent cotton button-down shirts, pleated and double-pleated slacks, and penny loafers. Oh, and madras—lots of madras. By my thirties, I collected at least a dozen fabric watchbands in just about every color combination, and each morning I'd mix and match them with my gingham shirts in a rainbow of colors and my ribbon belts embroidered with sailboats, dolphins, and hounds.

By the time I hit the mid-century mark, however, I began to feel the invisibility that comes with age. I'd read some online advice that cautioned, "The older you get, the more people will want to pretend you're invisible. Don't let them." Then came the call to arms: "Don't be afraid to startle," with this admonition: "[Wear] whatever it takes to remind people that you're there and, if necessary, that you're older and wiser than them."

A good friend, just a few years younger than I am, is cut from the same cloth as Mom and me. Deon and I both liked actress Heather (*Twin Peaks*) Graham, who once told an interviewer, "I admire those people who hold on to their elegance in old age, but I'd rather have fun." Like me, Deon also claimed a genetic sartorial link, in his case to his great-great-aunt Mae, who was known for her bright red lipstick and loud, floral-print dresses. Aunt Mae, to hear Deon describe her, was "no wallflower." When he entered his fifties, Deon explained, "I didn't want be that 'old dude' trying to wear something from Hollister or Abercrombie & Fitch, but I also wasn't ready to consign myself to wearing Dockers all the time, either." His goal? To have clothes that are just a little bit better than everyone else's. It gives the younger guys something to emulate.

Before we ended our chat, Deon reminded me of what Coco Chanel once said: "Fashion changes, but style endures."

Hear, hear, Deon!

After I wrote about vanity in *The New York Times*, I quickly heard from a woman in her sixties who posted in the comments: "I started to realize that lack of attention to appearance makes a person (of any age) look older and it radiates a loud message, 'It's hopeless, why bother.' Or, on the worst days, 'this building is condemned.'" She told me that one day, she caught a reflection of herself in the mirror that served as a wake-up call. "I vowed to clean up my act, and to dress with dignity. Every day. It's one of the best decisions I ever made. Dressing with dignity boosts my self-esteem and makes me feel younger. I embrace my age with pride."

Mom would have understood "dressing with dignity," although with her own twist. As a lifelong reader, she'd long been a fan of the British poet Jenny Joseph, whose much-loved poem, "Warning," speaks of wearing purple with a red hat and living freely and fully to compensate for a youth of "sobriety."

Of course, Mom had no need to make up for any sobriety of her own youth—as her memorable wedding dress reminded me.

I Won't Limit Myself
to Friends My Own Age

Surrounding yourself with other people your own age is a surefire strategy for feeling old. Thankfully, I had the perfect ninety-something role model for making and keeping friends who are decades younger than I am.

S OME OF DENISE KESSLER'S BEST FRIENDS were thirty or forty years younger than she, and I happily counted myself among them. When we met in 1993, she was seventy-seven, and I had just turned thirty-six. You could say I was her "Harold" (a young man bored with his life but obsessed with death) and she my "Maude" (an old woman living life to its fullest and charged with vitality). Talk about a mismatched couple.

Denise chose me. Initially, I assumed she'd picked me solely based on my FICO score, since I'd applied to rent the garden apartment beneath hers. I came to understand—fairly quickly—that becoming a tenant of Denise's was step one to becoming a friend. Few made the cut, but those of us who did had one thing in common: our age. Sure, Denise had some septuagenarian friends, but as she once told me, she had "little patience for old people."

She also had little time for them, or anyone, and she struggled to find an hour to interview me for the flat. Her days were chock full: water aerobics in the morning, copy editing the local paper later in the day, attending street demonstrations anytime, writing letters to the editor often, and donning her wig to join her feminist sisters in the Last Hoo-Rahs ("a cheerleading brigade and authentic barefoot hula-tap troupe") that performed at birthdays, graduations, and other parties—always exiting to a standing ovation.

Denise did have blood relatives, but she wasn't especially close to most of them (with the exception of her granddaughter, whom she adored), and she had her own definition of family. To paraphrase *Tales of the City* novelist Armistead Maupin, Denise created her family of "logicals" rather than rely on her "biologicals." Maupin later titled his memoir *Logical Family*, explaining "that sometimes your biological family won't accept you at all, and you have to form your own circle of friends and loved ones who are logical for you."

Denise recruited her logicals, much as Maupin's fictional matriarch Anna Madrigal did, presiding over us as "both a spiritual guide and surrogate mother," as *The New York Times* described Mrs. Madrigal. We went on day trips to the coast and evening excursions to the theater; I taught her how to use email, the web, and finally her iPhone; and in later years, I ferried her to the doctor, the hospital, and, finally, the assisted living home. So, too, did her other beloved "logicals."

Her merry band of younger followers did more than help with errands. I believe we also helped combat the loneliness of advancing age, especially after her three sisters died. Denise had been the baby. "I was left behind," she mentioned to me more than a couple of times.

Long before the studies came out touting the benefits of having younger friends, Denise lived the life. I remember her telling me that "having younger friends opens your world up. They broaden your perspective." She also understood, intuitively, that close friendships in old age were a strong predictor of increased longevity and, yes, greater happiness.

Still, our twenty-year friendship proved far from one-sided. I valued nothing more than her ongoing life advice, handed out as though she were an endless Pez dispenser. As she benefited from the strength and vitality of her younger friends, we benefited from the wisdom and persistence she'd accrued with age. One day, still early in our friendship but after I'd moved out of Denise's house, the tree cutters came to prune an overgrown sycamore that provided a curtain of privacy in my backyard. I told the supervisor I'd be on a conference call, but to get me if he had a question.

An hour later, I went back to check on his progress, and I couldn't believe what I saw. "You've completely hacked the tree," I shouted. Desolate, because my neighbors now had a perfect line of sight into my bedroom, I phoned Denise, hoping for some grandmotherly consolation. Instead, she told me, right out of the "tough love" playbook: "If something matters to you, you need to pay attention to it." That's a life lesson that applies to more than trees.

Thanks to Denise's example, by my forties I'd begun to enlarge my circle with younger friends—some of them ten, even twenty years younger than me. Take Daryl, whom I hired as an editorial assistant right after he graduated from college. A decade later he helped me set up my first email address, create my first PowerPoint, and even taught me basic HTML coding. Without him I'd never have gotten my first job as a digital journalist.

Others I know are also on similar searches. "My younger friends definitely give me a sense of energy and excitement," a fifty-something friend explained. "They have insight into what is more important in the world now that wasn't important when I was young. They have hopes, dreams, and goals that my older friends just don't have the energy for." Others touched on the optimism of their Millennial and Gen Z friends. "It's so easy to feel jaded and cynical as one grows older," my friend Jack told me, "but people in their twenties, especially college students, remain stubbornly optimistic. They *will* change the world—even if our generation has largely messed up the globe."

And don't forget the tangible, even fun, benefits of younger friends. "They are more likely to stay out late," and "They have a willingness to do new things," I've heard repeatedly. A colleague at *Time* magazine recounted with glee, "They tell me how to write an SEO headline that actually attracts readers!" Then, natch, they are built-in tech support, much as I'd been for Denise and as Daryl had been for me. Not too long ago, I asked my then nineteen-year-old niece Caroline how to embed a hyperlink into a Word document. Done! Other contemporaries have told me, almost rapturously, how they've learned to tweet, use Instagram, clear their cache, and upgrade their privacy settings thanks to the younger people in their midst. One boasted: "Just the other day I found out the meaning of 'TIL.'" Clueless as to what that meant, I asked for its meaning: "Today I learned." Aha!

Sure, younger friends are less experienced, sometimes even irritating. Some "never stop staring at their phones." Then there is the ongoing devolution of the English language into emojis, avatars, and acronyms. But I try to remember what really matters: connection, not convention.

It's also about attitude. Over and over, I've witnessed how my contemporaries speak down to younger people, belittling their values and experiences. One Millennial posted online: "You cannot expect young people to respect you when you are not prepared to respect them. Show younger people genuine respect and you'll have younger friends."

Finally, there's also a selfish reason to bridge these divides. New research shows that these "intergenerational" friendships provide value to all, with friendship itself positively impacting physical health and psychological well-being. One large study found that people with solid friendships have a 50 percent greater likelihood of survival compared to those with poor social relationships. How important is this? The study's authors determined that having friends "is comparable with quitting smoking, and it exceeds many well-known risk factors for mortality (e.g., obesity, physical inactivity)." To have friends well into old age, you need them to be younger than you!

That's why I've chosen to identify as a "Perennial," a term coined by tech entrepreneur Gina Pell to describe "ever-blooming, relevant people of all ages who live in the present time, know what's happening in the world, stay current with technology, and have friends of all ages. Perennials get involved, stay curious, mentor others, and are passionate, compassionate, creative, confident, collaborative, global-minded risk takers, and who know how to hustle." Millennials can be Perennials. Boomers can be Perennials. Anyone can choose to be a Perennial.

Make no mistake, my friend Denise was a Perennial, putting off her "Last Hoo-Rah" until the age of ninety-eight. And when she left the stage in 2015, I was glad to be there with all of her friends, every one of us younger than she, to give her a final standing ovation.

I Won't Lie
About My Age
(Even on Dating Apps)

I used to be one of those people who shaved a few years (or more) off their true age—either to avoid appearing like a dinosaur or to improve their odds of finding a match online. But no more. Now, I'm out and proud about the years I've logged.

Six months after I separated from my husband, I joined Tinder, one of the many dating apps available to singles ready to mingle. Soon enough I found a match: "Michael," who gave his age as fifty. I recognized him right away, since he'd been a college classmate of mine. He was fifty the way I was fifty-seven on my profile (which is to say we were both sixty at the time). I had to admit he looked great for sixty, but his forehead crevices and droopy eyelids did him no favors as a fifty-year-old. Michael should have taken the advice once given to me: add seven years to your age and then people will be amazed at how good you look.

I chatted with Michael, asking how his subterfuge—okay, let's call it lying—was working out for him. He explained, seriously, "It's not the number that matters. It's the appearance and energy of youth. If you don't act like a crabby man online, you can be any age you want." That really didn't answer my question, which I re-asked, and he replied. "Half the guys I meet get up and walk out on me when I tell them I'm actually sixty," he said. "But half of them don't—and getting in the door is all that matters."

To be honest, I don't have his chutzpah. That's one reason I've stopped lying about my age. I'd like to say that's all about my quest for authenticity, but I'll admit it also has to do with the Internet ratting me out.

Frankly, it used to be so easy to lie . . . or just not tell the truth. Ten years ago, when I was in my early fifties and didn't yet have a Wikipedia page, which shouts your actual birthday in the first line of the entry, I remember nodding my head in agreement when a fellow writer asked if I were "in my forties, too." In fact, I already had my AARP membership card, but I saw no reason to dispute his generous assumption, especially since I was surrounded by a cadre of his contemporaries. This wasn't lying; it was merely a sin of omission.

Then came the separation, followed by my divorce. I turned sixty—entering the decade of life known as "sexagenarian," which I like to joke is all about sex. As I mentioned, I joined Tinder (and Match, OkCupid, and some other dating services), and with a single click (or two, or three) I became three years younger. I was a fifty-something again, or what I call mid-century modern.

On most apps, fibbing proved easy enough—I just se-
lected 1960 instead of 1957 as my birth year. Tinder
proved more complicated, since it pulls profile data from
Facebook, where I was sixty. That meant I had to change
my birth year on Facebook, too—and then mark it as private, since many people on that platform know my real
age. (I'd decided it was okay to fib about my age to
strangers, but I didn't actually want to be unmasked as a
liar to people I know.)

I knew it was important to be proud and honest about
my age, and that my purported birth year was a lie. But
there are liars, and then there are LIARS (or so I told myself), and I simply wanted to be matched with people in
the right age-group. After all, I heard that voice in my
head: "Who could be looking for a guy in his sixties?"

Like my college classmate Michael, I justified my fibbing—in two different ways. First, if I were to use my
real age and the man of my dreams set his search pa-
rameters to a maximum of fifty-nine, he'd be shown
candidates in their fifties—but he would miss me. A
single friend who is fifty-four and has some experience
in this game told me: "A lot of people restrict their
searches to people within a certain age range. So I say
put whatever age you want, but disclose before you
meet the person. If the true age is a barrier, you're wasting everyone's time. However, if fudging gets you in the
door—and then you're honest about it BEFORE wasting
someone's time—then no harm, no foul." There it was,
that same phrase Michael had used—"getting in the
door"—which is another way to say the end justifies the
means. For the record: this second friend is a lawyer

and has never suffered in making a persuasive argument—even when wrong.

The other reason I justified my fibbing? I wasn't nearly as bad as the fellow described by at twenty-six-year-old woman in an online rant. She went to the coffee shop expecting to meet the man in the photo she saw online: blond, early thirties, nice abs. But when she looked around the shop, the only man who was alone and obviously waiting for someone was in his sixties, sporting gray hair and a fleshy midsection. She was furious; this man clearly thought his date wouldn't notice that he'd lied through his teeth. (Apparently, she did notice.)

Or should I say, *we* notice.

To be fair, though, sometimes it's not so much lying as self-delusion. In my own mind, I'm still a dead ringer for forty-five, and more than once I've been caught by surprise when I see myself in a mirror. I'm sure I wasn't the only one thrown for a loop by that Facebook "10-year Challenge" (where you posted a photo of your current self, side by side with one from a decade ago), making me wonder how I'd changed so much without having noticed it. Cue Doris Lessing, who wrote, "The great secret that all old people share is that you really haven't changed in seventy or eighty years. Your body changes, but you don't change at all."

Let's be real, though—it's not only men who lie. A fellow who didn't give his name told Metro News, "I had a date with a flight attendant whose profile said she was forty-five. Only when she arrived, it turned out she was fifty-five, and she looked every bit of it." He was further put off when she was very blasé about her fabrication.

She told him that she liked younger men and didn't want to scare them off.

While I was still in my fibbing stage, I made it a policy to disclose my real age the first time I met someone face-to-face, no matter if it had taken a white lie "to get in the door." Unlike Michael's experience, I never had anyone give me the stink eye and turn on his heels. But I remember one time, I was chatting online with a university professor (who claimed he was fifty-six) when he asked me out of the blue, "What's your real age?" and accused me of lying. Alas, I had already told him my real name, which he had Googled (of course), and he found my Wiki page, which shouted: STEVEN PETROW IS SIXTY. I didn't even have time to reply before he asked how he could trust me about anything else I'd told him. "Well, you could read my full Wikipedia page," I wanted to say, but it didn't matter. He had already blocked me.

I never did find out *his* real age.

Lots of online daters have grown wise to fibbers and have learned to work lie-detecting questions into early conversations to squirrel out a match's real age. My sixty-year-old college mate Michael told me he'd created a cheat sheet to help him answer the most frequently asked questions during early texting (while still maintaining his fiction of being ten years younger). While we were both born in 1957, he needed to talk about his life as though he had been born in 1967.

That can be tricky to keep track of. If someone asked Michael if he remembered the JFK assassination, he'd have to do some quick thinking to know that his fake younger self hadn't yet been born in 1963. If someone asked, "Where were you when you heard about the Americans being taken hostage in Iran?" he might unthinkingly answer that he had just started medical school. (If he were really ten years younger, he would have been in middle school for that 1979 event.)

It's true what they say about lying being hard work—there's an awful lot to remember once you start to weave that tangled web.

In the end, because of my discomfort with lying (and that damned Wiki page), I decided to try an experiment. Using the same photos, I listed three different ages on three different dating apps to see if it would it make a difference. After six months, I had my answer: No, it didn't. For guys in their fifties or sixties, I was "age appropriate" no matter my stated age. For men looking for a "daddy," I qualified every single time. And for those younger guys who didn't want an "old" fellow, I couldn't even get a woof.

I'm now my real age on all the apps—except one. Tinder still lists me as three years younger. I've tried to fix it, I really have, but Tinder won't let you change your age once you've created an account. My written profile says it's a mistake, but anyone searching by age will still find the "younger" me. But hey, sometimes there's only so much truth-telling a person can do.

I Won't Join the
"Organ Recital"

It starts out innocently enough—you sympathize with a friend who's had minor surgery, or mention your own high blood pressure diagnosis. A few short years later, every social event becomes a chorus of sticky joints, cataracts, or way worse.

I T CAN HAPPEN ANYWHERE, at any gathering, any time a few people of a certain age get together. First the fanfare: "What's new with you?" Then the overture: the high cholesterol, the prediabetes, and the bum knee. Before you know it, the music swells and it's a full-blown concert of sciatica, angina, and replacement joints. Welcome to the front row of the worst musical revue imaginable. Yes, you're at an "organ recital."

Even worse, in my experience, is the group singalong: One person mentions a health condition, another chimes in to one-up the first, and rather quickly, you are entwined in an endless tragicomedy about every ailment from bunions to shingles, cataracts to kidney stones, cancer to heart disease. Boomers, like me, can't stop talking about ourselves—even as we're falling apart. All too many of us are sadly under the delusion that this is appropriate conversation—interesting, even. Friends: It is not. Please kk that. (That's internet slang for "okay" or "I got it.")

Here's one of my worst such recitals. Not long ago, I went out on a first date with a nice, good-looking fellow. Oh, and he was "age appropriate" (which is anyone older than half your age plus seven years). First dates are supposed to be the taster course in the relationship world, but instead of whetting my appetite for more, he left me quite sated by the end of the evening. In fact, I became a hostage to his monologue of medical mishaps: "I probably didn't tell you on the phone about my repetitive strain injury, two joint replacements, failing eyesight, high triglycerides, and low blood pressure—not to mention I have a congenital condition I inherited from my mother . . ." Taking forever to make a selection from the menu, he prattled on: "I am extremely squeamish and weird about some meats, fish, and chicken. I realize my food issues are strange and unreasonable . . ." *Uh-huh*, I nodded. Somewhere between the amuse-bouche and the main dish—let's call it an intermezzo—he revealed he'd recently had prostate cancer and that the surgery had left him impotent. "But don't worry," he continued, "I can inject prostaglandin [a hormone] directly into my penis and have a full erection in minutes." Too. Much. Information.

How did this happen? It wasn't that long ago that we—allegedly the most self-absorbed, if not downright narcissistic, generation in the history of humankind—talked incessantly about our kids ("Am I biased, or is my child really the best?"), our vacations ("We are #blessed to be visiting nirvana"), and our jobs ("I got my full bonus this year. How about you?").

Not that I've developed full immunity myself. While I won't use #blessed to describe my vacations or #house-beautiful for my old-timey cottage, I have posted a lot of travel and house photos. And you know what they say: Tell me what you brag about and I'll tell you what you lack. And this: a picture is worth a thousand hashtags. All this boils down to one thing:

Me. Me. Me.

So, is the organ recital really so different than this?

Not entirely. It is, after all, an extension of our life-long self-absorption. But here's the rub: The more we define ourselves by our frailties and illnesses, the more we allow them to become us. I may *have* cardiovascular disease, but I *am not* my cardiovascular disease. As much as depression leaves its imprint on me, I will not let it define me. Meet me for the first time, and I hope you'll learn a lot of other things before you hear about my numerous aches and pains—or high coronary calcium score.

Take the date I described at the beginning of this chapter. By the end of dinner, I knew nothing about his work, his relationships, his family, or his joys and sadnesses. All I knew was his medical record, in excruciating detail. Frankly, I think the only thing he left out was his blood type—which I'm sure he would have revealed if I'd stayed for dessert. I didn't.

Yes, illness is part of our lives, and I'm all for disclosure when it comes to what ails us. Talking openly about *serious* diseases and conditions can be hugely helpful. After suffering from depression for decades, I finally acknowledged it to others when I was fifty-nine. Yes, fifty-nine. As I told friends—and then disclosed publicly— the suicide of my friend Erik, who had long endured severe depression but never told anyone—proved to be the catalyst. I wrote in an essay, "As a health journalist, I have often used my own stories to write about difficult-to-discuss medical conditions, including learning I had testicular cancer at age twenty-six and my misdiagnosis with HIV/AIDS—back when it was a death sentence. But I had never written about suffering from depression, even though it's plagued me since I first put pen to paper at age eleven, when I started keeping a diary."

I found so much relief in sharing this part of me with others. Even more rewarding, friends—sometimes strangers—still email me (years later) to talk about their mental health issues. I know I'm no therapist, but I'm glad to have done my small part to lessen the stigma and loneliness.

If a friend gets a frightening diagnosis, I want to hear about it so I can offer a supportive ear—or a doctor referral. I hope I can count on others to do the same for me. But please, let's make a strong correlation between the severity of a disease and the amount of time spent talking about it.

I want to know the joys of *good* health news, too. Recently, a Millennial friend, who could teach us Boomers a lot, shared on Facebook the saga of her many painful and unsuccessful attempts at in vitro fertilization. Hurrah! She had finally become pregnant, posting: "We asked for prayers back in December, and God heard all of your sweet prayers LOUD and clear. We are so grateful and blessed to announce that after 2 long years of trying, our baby GIRL will be born in September."

The challenge is to find the line between "not enough" and "too much," to know the distinction between run-of-the-mill ailments and serious illness, and to know our audience.

I promise to do my part: I won't make a show of taking my meds at a dinner gathering, or announce to everyone at a cocktail party that I'm due for a follow-up EKG. I will limit any talk of routine aches and pains to just one cocktail. And I'll do my best to stop the music when I hear the opening notes of a cacophony. We are more than the sum of our organs.

I Won't Deny
That I'm Slow to Rise
(and I'm Okay with That)

By our age, it should not surprise anyone that men (and many women) might have some issues with sexual function, but that doesn't mean we can't be sexual or intimate anymore. Touch matters!

ASK A ROOMFUL OF MEN fifty-five plus whether they have any kind of sexual dysfunction—such as problems with erections, sex drive, or overall satisfaction—and at least half should raise their hand, studies suggest. They probably won't, since the topic is fraught with stigma, shame, and fear of rejection.

That's cold comfort to people like me, because—if I were to be honest—I would have to raise my own hand.

I didn't have to wait until I was sixty, though, to join this particular club. I got in about thirty-five years ago—call it "early admission"—as a side effect of cancer surgery. Picture me then, a young grad student sitting on a cold examination table in a hospital gown that didn't quite cover my backside. Having just confirmed my testicular cancer diagnosis, the oncologist went on to tell me about a common side effect called "retrograde, or dry ejaculation," in which things don't flow where they should during sex. Semen, instead of exiting my body during an orgasm, would spill into my bladder. The doctor assured me that it wouldn't diminish my sexual pleasure, but he had no suggestions about how to share such news with new intimates.

I was in my twenties at the time, and I felt completely alone. Sexual dysfunction isn't often a young man's issue, and this was long before there were online support groups for every disease known to humankind.

My oncologist's prediction about the side effect, as well as his assurance about sexual pleasure, both turned out to be true. It didn't really matter much at first because I entered a years-long period of celibacy in which I tried to get comfortable with this "new normal." I also feared that disclosure would put a swift end to any new sexual relationship. That never happened. At my age then, I was less confident in myself and certainly didn't have the language to explain my condition, especially when romancing. Eventually, through trial, error, and time, I did find my words, often adding—with a touch of humor—that I offered "no muss, no mess sex," which also was "safer sex."

"For many of these treatments, whether it's surgery or radiation, and whether it's prostate cancer or bladder cancer, about 85 percent of men will report some difficulty with [sexual functioning]," Christian Nelson, chief of the psychiatry service at Memorial Sloan Kettering Cancer Center, told me. "The most prominent sexual dysfunction we see related to those treatments are difficulty with erections, or erectile dysfunction." he added.

Nelson wasn't surprised to learn I had been celibate for a number of years after surgery. He has learned that when things don't work as they should, for many men "there's upset and sometimes shame... that can lead to avoidance." His practice helps guys identify and use the medications and penile injections that will "help them reengage sexually, reengage in dating, reengage in intimacy."

I wish this kind of help had been available to me when I needed it most.

But you don't need cancer treatment to get into the sexual dysfunction club. Admission can be granted through smoking, diabetes, or hypertension, but mainly through growing older, says Brant Inman, the codirector of Duke Cancer Institute's Center for Prostate and Urologic Cancer, who has studied male sexual function. The usual cause of age-related dysfunction, he explained, is vascular, meaning "impaired blood flow to the penis." In other words, even if I hadn't been granted early entry into the club, my membership card probably would have arrived anyway, as predictably as that AARP card.

I spoke with several men about these issues, all of whom asked me not to use their names for privacy reasons. One of them, a sixty-year-old art dealer from Manhattan, told me he hasn't been able to achieve an erection for years, which he finds "incredibly frustrating and embarrassing." He says he tells partners that it's because of his meds, which it may well be (he has taken

antidepressants that can have sexual effects). One partner told him, "It's not the destination that's important. It's
the journey"—a gentle acceptance that, as he put it,
helped him to relax.

A fifty-year-old advertising executive said he was too
embarrassed to talk to his doctor about erectile problems that had begun to plague him and instead bought
Cialis and Viagra from a friend. The medication helped
somewhat, but he still couldn't reach orgasm—and even
then, he wasn't comfortable talking to his doctor about it,
given that he'd obtained his drugs through such unortho-
dox channels.

Inman says he understands the embarrassment, but
asked, rhetorically, "Would you buy your cholesterol or
blood pressure–lowering medication from a street ven-
dor?" Of course not, he says, because you can't be sure of
the dosage (milligrams of active agent) or quality (active
agent versus filler), which could be dangerous. He en-
courages men to be completely frank with their doctors
in order to get the best care.

It's not just with doctors, however, that full disclosure
can be fraught for men experiencing sexual dysfunction.
When and how to tell a new partner feels like a big issue.
Before undressing? Post-intimacy? It depends, Memorial
Sloan Kettering's Nelson says.

It's certainly easy enough to take a pill without telling
your partner, the psychiatrist told me; treatments, such
as shots to help with an erection, require more finesse if
not disclosure. "I certainly have some men who haven't
told new partners that they use injections," Nelson says.
"They step into a bathroom, inject, and ten minutes later

they engage in sexual relations." But he recommends a discussion beforehand when someone plans to use an injection—both so there are no last-minute surprises and to reduce the secrecy, which often covers for shame.

Sometimes, being frank about your own sexual dysfunction leads to a discovery that you're not alone. That's what happened to me with a man I dated for a while. After we had gotten to know each other, but before we'd taken our clothes off, he told me he'd had prostate cancer surgery and needed penile injections to have sex. "That seemed like a good time for me to have this conversation," he explained later, but his trust in me led me to talk about my own condition. The result was a deeper level of intimacy, which I've come to learn is another way to gauge sexual satisfaction.

I don't presume to have the same level of insight into older women's sexual issues as I do into men's, but I know the challenges of aging don't just affect men, and these problems can be equally awkward for women to talk about. Sexual dysfunction in women, which also becomes more common with age, includes vaginal dryness, pain during intercourse, and a decrease in both arousal and ability to reach orgasm. Unfortunately, despite chatter about a "female Viagra," there is not yet the medical equivalent of an impotence medication, a pump, or an injection to treat women.

That is not to say that women don't want to continue to have sex well into their older years. Demographics are against them, with women outnumbering men starting at age forty—and by eighty-five, there are five women for every man in the United States. Nevertheless, they persist, with sisters often doing it for themselves (and with each other).

One of my favorite story lines on the Netflix series *Grace and Frankie* focuses on the lead characters' development of a vibrator designed specifically for older women. Lily Tomlin and Jane Fonda, the now eighty-something costars, get to work on what they call "Ménage à Moi" after Fonda's "Grace" develops carpal tunnel from her existing vibrator. Special features include its soft-grip gel sleeve, extra-large glow-in-the dark control buttons ("so you don't have to wreck your arthritic wrists"), and an easy-angle tip. Said Fonda about the story line, "It gives us hope. It makes us less afraid to get older." I hope it also gave them more pleasure.

All I can say is, when it comes to sexual performance and satisfaction, none of us should have to give it up, whatever our age. I've also learned that what gave me pleasure as a young man is very different than what does today. My vow: I won't hesitate to ask for what I need, and will embrace it as equally satisfying, just different.

I Won't Avoid Looking at Myself Naked in the Mirror

I bear a noticeable reminder of my long-ago cancer surgery, what I call "the scar." It's taken a few decades to learn to accept it, even take some pride in it, and I promise I won't hide it from future partners—or myself.

MY PERSONAL TRAINER, KARI, had me down on the mat in the middle of a tough set of obliques when my T-shirt rode up and revealed it. "It" is a twelve-inch-long scar that runs from below my navel to my breastbone. Kari didn't hesitate to ask, "What's up with your scar?"

"My" scar—and I do feel proprietary about it—has been a part of me for more than three decades. Still, an answer to Kari's question doesn't come easily. At first, I thought I would just pretend I hadn't heard the question, but she knows my hearing is fine. I briefly considered telling her a flat-out lie: "I was shot in the stomach." (This is not as far-fetched as it might sound; I once knew a guy with a similar scar on his belly that really was caused by a gunshot.) Finally, I settled on the truth. "It's from a long-ago cancer surgery," I explained, outing myself as a member of the "cancer club."

In 1984, after an eight-hour operation to remove cancerous lymph nodes from my abdominal cavity and two weeks spent recovering in the hospital, I went home with some extra painkillers, instructions for changing my surgical dressing, and my scar. It was actually a remarkable wound—sutured with silk, woven with wire, and zipped up with no-rust staples. At the time, I was single and twenty-six. All the years since then I've wrestled with how to come to terms with what my scar embodies and how to talk about it—especially when it comes to being intimate with someone new.

Early on, when the wound was still red and raw—and so visible, before the hair grew back on my chest and belly—I simply didn't want anyone to see it. I refused to take off my shirt in a locker room or at the beach. I didn't want to answer some form of Kari's "what's with the scar?" question.

I didn't want to see it, either. At home alone, I'd undress in a darkened room to make sure I didn't catch a glimpse. Every so often, I'd step out of the shower and see that rough-hewn line reflected in the medicine chest mirror, and it would set off an avalanche of emotion. It wasn't just the obvious disfigurement. The scar represented the loss of my younger self's sense of invulnerability, and—no surprise—it triggered a fear of recurrence, if not worse.

I didn't want to expose that scar, or those feelings, to anyone, and as it turns out, those inclinations are common. Dr. Jeffrey Marcus, the chief of pediatric plastic surgery at Duke University, who has treated thousands of patients in his twenty-year tenure, told me that we all have very personal responses to disfigurements like scars. "A scar is a physical deformity, it's a physical difference," he explained, adding that scars ignite questions of identity because other people "tend to draw conclusions or make assumptions about attractiveness, intelligence, even capability based on something they see."

I felt sure that others would use the scar to judge not just my appearance but my sexual prowess. Being single presented a wrenching set of dilemmas. What was I supposed to do when going to bed with someone for the first time? Nothing breaks the mood like announcing, "Hey, I have a really big scar because I had cancer!" After a few awkward test drives with potential boyfriends, I chose to be celibate for a couple of years. (Those sexual side effects of the cancer played a big part in my celibacy as well.)

When I finally rebooted my dating practice, I made sure to keep the lights low—if not off—and sported a tank top in bed. I hoped to pass for shy rather than ashamed. Most of my dates were decent men, or maybe they were myopic, or maybe they were shy themselves.

One fellow didn't take more than two breaths before saying goodbye after he asked me about the scar. But it wasn't the optics of the scar, or the sexual aftereffects; it was the cancer itself. "I just buried my partner who died from cancer," he said. "I can't go down that path again." The Americans with Disabilities Act may protect people with cancer (and other serious illnesses) from discrimination on the job, but we're on our own in the bedroom.

By my mid-thirties, the scar had softened and faded. Along the way, my shame had morphed into true shyness, and then I began toddling toward acceptance: I came out by taking off my shirt at the beach. I got naked in the bedroom. I actually looked at myself in the mirror. And in my late forties, I got married, scar and all. Acceptance and self-acceptance.

What had once been a stark reminder of my illness had become something else altogether. It had become a testament to my survival. Reading Cormac McCarthy's *All the Pretty Horses* one afternoon, I stopped in recognition when I came upon this line: "Scars have the strange power to remind us that our past is real."

My scar had become a talisman of sorts, a visual and lasting connection to my own history. As Dr. Jeff Marcus, the plastic surgeon, told me, "Some differences can be positive, too."

Then, after fourteen years together, my husband and I divorced. Once again, I found myself in the dating market. Older, for sure. Wiser, still to be determined. But I have noticed a silver lining of sorts. Potential boyfriends—at least, those my age—live with all sorts of scars, from open-heart surgery to various cancers and sports-related procedures. Along with age-related sexual dysfunction, this is the new normal. Yay, gray!

Sure, I still have some unease about it from time to time. But decades after my surgery, I keep coming back to this realization: My scar is visible proof that I have survived. Without it, I could not be whole. It is, literally, what binds me together. Time may heal all wounds—if not all scars—and that's just fine with me.

Go ahead, ask me to take my clothes off. I'll likely say yes.

I Won't Become a Miserable Malcontent, a Cranky Curmudgeon, or a Surly Sourpuss

When I was younger, a funny but wise cancer nurse reminded me how important it is to keep laughter handy even in dark days. I promise to look for the humorous side of getting older rather than slip into the role of grumpy old man.

I LOVE MEL BROOKS. Full stop. *Young Frankenstein. High Anxiety.* I could go on forever—just as he seems to; he's ninety-four years old at the time of this writing. What's his secret? "Humor keeps the elderly rolling along, singing a song. When you laugh, it's a voluntary explosion of the lungs. So you laugh, you breathe, the blood runs, and everything is circulating. If you don't laugh, you die."

I wasn't dying, but I sure wasn't laughing, either, when I was admitted to Memorial Sloan Kettering Cancer Center in 1984. I was so scared I wet myself. And I wasted no time picking an argument with the nurse—not about the following day's eight-hour surgery but about the inferior quality of the sheets on my narrow hospital bed. It started when she warned me what the next day would bring: "You better get some sleep now, because tomorrow you're going to feel like a Mack truck rode over you in first gear and reverse." While I knew I was being pretentious, even ridiculous under the circumstances, my 400-thread-Egyptian-cotton-or-better self asked, "How can I expect to get a good night's sleep on cotton/polyester blend sheets?" (I'd yet to learn that a good night's sleep is not remotely part of the hospital experience.) The nurse replied matter-of-factly, "You better focus your energy on what really matters."

Then she added with a playful wink, "Those 'cotton/poly' sheets? There's not a stitch of cotton in them. They're actually one hundred percent polyester."

She began to laugh. As did my parents, who were there with me. Finally, I was overcome, too. The endorphin release triggered by the nurse's playfulness fell over us like a game of happy hormone dominoes.

It's now been more than four decades since Norman Cousins led a revolution and urged patients, in collaboration with their doctors, to use humor to boost their bodies' capacity for healing. Cousins had been diagnosed with a crippling and irreversible disease for which there was no known cure. As all else failed, Cousins, best known for the phrase "laughter is the best medicine," turned to his still-potent sense of humor to prove what an effective healing tool the mind can provide.

His landmark book, *Anatomy of an Illness: As Perceived by the Patient*, published five years before my diagnosis, had been given to me early on by my friend Helena along with an admonition "to find your inner funny." I replied that "there's nothing humorous about my situation." Helena's answer: "Read the book"—which I did, promptly falling in love with Cousins and his message of laughter and hope. I still have my original 1979 edition, with sections underlined, like these two:

> Ten minutes of genuine belly laughter had an anesthetic effect and would give me at least two hours of pain-free sleep.

> Laughter may or may not activate the endorphins or enhance respiration, as some medical researchers contend. What seems clear, however, is that laughter is an antidote to apprehension and panic.

In the years since his book was published, science has proven Cousins right, documenting that laughter is indeed a potent endorphin releaser. (For science nerds: It activates the release of the neurotransmitter serotonin—the same brain chemical boosted by the most common type of antidepressant, SSRIs. Serotonin reduces pain, increases job performance, connects people emotionally, and improves the flow of oxygen to the heart and brain. Serotonin makes us feel happy.)

Of course, it can be really hard to laugh—or keep any sense of humor—when you're anxious, hurting, or scared. But the reverse is true as well. Try laughing and feeling afraid at the same time. It's impossible. My nurse at

Memorial Sloan Kettering knew just that when she glee-fully told me that my hospital sheets were the finest polyester made. Laughing at myself broke the grip of fear, and made it easier to face what was coming.

Humor—especially about illness, or worse, impend-ing death—is tricky business. I remember a few years ago when *Conan* comedy writer Laurie Kilmartin began tweeting about her father's last days to her tens of thousands of followers. The tweets she sent from his hospital bedside were laced with Kilmartin's trademark dark humor ("For Valentine's Day, I got my Dad a gift card from JCPenney. I said, 'Dad, I want this card to ex-pire before you do'") and authenticity ("Hard to leave Dad's side. I am drawn to him like a moth to a flame—that's about to go out").

When her father died, Kilmartin took to Twitter with this sincere post: "Hey, all, Dad passed away about an hour ago. Thanks for all your messages, he was bowled over that so many strangers were thinking of him." But it wasn't long before she took to joking again in her tweets: "Do I correct the friend who wrote 'condolences on loos-ing your father'?" she posted. (Yep, friend, that's "losing.")

Kilmartin's father allowed for such humor. So did my mom, mostly, who approached her last years with good cheer and good humor. Each morning when Mom read *The Times*, she'd jump right to the obits. One day, she threw down the paper in disgust, shouting, "Jesus Christ! I'm so old, I don't even know any of these people." Later, as the end came closer and Mom took a bad turn, she said to me, "I think I'm really dying." To which I re-plied, "You mean today? Because I'm going to the supermarket, so if you really think so, I won't shop for you." "That's hilarious," she countered. "What's for dinner?"

I've pored over a lot of those "guilty as charged" studies that maintain older people are crabby, humorless. "No Joke: Sense of Humor Declines with Age," declares one headline. Another claimed, "We laugh twice as much in our teens as we do in our fifties." (I know I did, but that was mostly because I was stoned for much of my teen years.) That lead researcher, who I sure wouldn't want as a dining companion, continued, "And our findings suggest that it's all downhill from 52."

I actually think playwright George Bernard Shaw had it right when he said, "We don't stop playing because we grow old, we grow old because we stop playing." I vow to keep laughing as long as I continue to breathe, even as it gets harder for me to do both of those things at once.

I Won't Pass Up a Chance to Pee (Even When I Don't Have To)

Legend has it that Queen Elizabeth II has said one of the keys to a monarch's success is never passing up a chance to use the loo. With the urge calling me a lot more frequently than it once did, I will take that advice to heart (and bladder).

UNTIL I HIT MY FIFTIES, I was a pretty ordinary urinator, especially if you're keeping count. My urologist, a very nice Canadian, tells me the normal number of times to pee is about six times a day, so our annual total comes to just under 2,200 "voids," and for years, I was hitting the mark.

In my younger days, I never paid any attention to any of this. I slept through the night without waking to go to the bathroom. I could fly from coast to coast—in a middle seat—and never get up to use the lavatory. Not that I mean to boast, but I simply had no problem in that department. Until I became a quinquagenarian, that is.

Yes, by my fifties, I had early signs that the times, they were a-changing. I tried to ignore them for a good long while, but then I started getting up once, then twice in a night "to go." Eventually I realized I had a problem and made sure to pee before bed.

Soon enough, I'd be certain "to go" before driving to work (or driving just about anywhere); right before the curtain at the theater; and twice, if possible, before wheels-up on a flight (cutting down on my preflight caffeine intake helped, as did handing over a few extra dollars for an aisle seat). I started paying attention to those road signs—"60 miles to the next rest stop"—on the interstate; if it were more than twenty minutes away, I would stop even if I didn't feel the urge yet.

Then came the day when I miscalculated. Driving from the Mojave Desert to Los Angeles International Airport on the I-10, a distance of about 150 miles, I decided to skip my mid-trip "safety pee" because, thanks to lane closures and car crashes, I was running way late. In bumper-to-bumper traffic, I crept toward LAX. I could feel my bladder first start to bulge, then crest like a river on the verge of a breach. I focused on all the perineum-strengthening exercises—basically Kegels—I'd done in yoga to build up my pelvic floor. I'd count, "one, two, three, four, five" and squeeze my pelvic muscles. Then, I'd release, also to a count of five. I had barely finished the second set when I knew I needed a better way.

I reached for my now empty water bottle (*Why did I drink so much?* I berated myself) to use as a makeshift "pee cup." Let me just say this, for the record: It is not easy to unzip oneself and urinate into a narrow-mouthed plastic bottle while driving a car in stop-and-go traffic. Not easy. And not at all tidy. "Never again," I vowed.

I wish I'd read the very helpful "How to Pee in a Bottle" *before* that day. WikiHow's step-by-step guide includes this necessary and basic advice:

- "Remember: it's better for a bottle to be too big than too small."
- "Sports drink bottles like Gatorade and Powerade tend to have a wider mouth."
- "You want to avoid being seen, as it is both embarrassing and illegal to expose yourself to others."

I confessed about my "wet nightmare" to my Facebook friends, who were quick to share all the times and places they make sure to plan ahead. I was relieved, so to speak, to hear that many of my contemporaries—both women and men—felt the same need to urinate more frequently.

Let's be clear: you never know when a potential leak lurks. As I learned, it might be on the I-10. Or, as others recounted: In the middle seat of a plane. On a subway. In a movie theater. At a play. During a worship service. On the way home from work, when the drawbridge is unexpectedly up.

That's why a music conductor I know always double-checks with himself ("Are you sure you don't need to go?") when he hears "maestro to the pit" just before stepping onto the podium to conduct an opera. And then there's a colleague, known for taking what he calls a "preventive pee," which served him especially well when he was "stuck in the Hyatt Vancouver's elevator for an hour and a half. I was relieved that I had just gone to the bathroom in my room."

Fortunately, the Internet is now chock-full of DIY solutions for this very problem. One fellow designed what he calls "a condom-catheter system," which consists of a gallon water jug, five feet of rubber tubing, a roll of duct tape, a condom, and some baby wipes. Apparently, his system worked in early clinical trials but failed in real-life situations. As he wrote, "It's not really super-comfortable to wear or use, and the penile-urine-soaking issue isn't ideal at all."

I give the final word to Queen Elizabeth, as is her due. According to an off-the-record palace source, Prince Charles, her firstborn and now seventy-two, was once asked by a reporter what the best advice the queen ever gave him on how to be a king. His answer: "Never pass up on an opportunity to use the loo." The royal septuagenarian speaks the truth.

I Won't Lie to My Doctor Anymore (Because These Lies Can Kill)

Doctor visits aren't much fun when they're all about what's falling apart, breaking down, and in need of repair. I may not agree with the advice I get, but I won't lie and tell my doctor I'm taking my meds, exercising, or sleeping well when I'm not actually doing any of those.

"**D**RUGS DON'T WORK IN PATIENTS who don't take them," former Surgeon General C. Everett Koop once said. It reminded me of how vexed I became when my father swore that he'd taken his blood pressure meds but had actually spit them into the toilet—which he forgot to flush, and which is where I found them. That afternoon, with Dad's systolic blood pressure at 180, in the danger zone, I had to call 911. "We're sending out an ambulance," the operator told me calmly. "He's a likely candidate for a major stroke." The paramedics rushed to the apartment and confirmed the dangerously high reading. At that point, Dad confessed what I already knew: he hadn't been taking his blood pressure medication after all.

As for my mom, I heard her tell the same bald-faced lie to her doctor time and again. "Mrs. Petrow, you're not smoking, are you?" "Of course not," she'd tell him. And then once home she'd go to her desk and pull out a deck of cards, as though intending to play solitaire. There were no cards, only cigarettes. It bothered her not a whit that she lied outright to her doctor about her single biggest health risk.

Alas, my parents were hardly outliers. People are notorious for lying to their doctors, and for not following their instructions. Studies have shown that, among older folks, 20 to 30 percent of all prescriptions are never filled and nearly half of all drugs for chronic conditions aren't taken as prescribed. Among those who do take them, they typically take only half of what the doctor prescribed, if they remember to take them at all. Sometimes they (or I should I say we?) will use an old prescription or borrow someone else's—without telling their doctor.

All kinds of reasons exist for this lack of compliance. Some of us just don't believe in taking medications, even for serious illness. Others believe we don't need to take them if we're feeling okay, or that they're just too costly (and let's be honest, depending on your health insurance, they can be prohibitively expensive). Some of my own friends confessed to me that they are among the noncompliant. A colleague blamed his memory: "I used to forget my blood pressure meds, but I started feeling buzzy headed, so I'm more careful now." Then she stopped taking her anti-seizure medication and had a stroke: "I hated being confined during the immediate stroke recovery and didn't ever want that again, so I always take my anti-seizure meds." That's a tough way to learn this lesson.

This lack of compliance (or what's also called adherence) can be deadly, totaling about 125 thousand lives a year and as much as 10 percent of hospitalizations.

Yes, I challenged my father to be more truthful with his doctors, acting as though I were a paragon of virtue, or of adherence, in this case. "You're only hurting yourself by skipping doses and not telling us," I high-and-mightied to him. Self-righteous when it came to his medication regimen, I paid scant attention to my own compliance. By age sixty, I had a pharmacopoeia of drugs in my medicine cabinet: Lipitor, Zetia, Niaspan, and baby aspirin (all for cardiovascular disease). Lexapro (for depression). And when needed, I'll swallow a blue Sonata (for sleeplessness) and a Klonopin (for anxiety), which—depending on the dose—come in many pretty colors: blue, yellow, white, green, and orange.

Whenever my doctors have asked me if I were taking all my medications, I've answered, "Yes." I wanted to be seen as a good patient. I did not want to be judged. But in reality, at the end of the month I'd skip days to stretch out an expensive prescription. For instance, all those heart drugs cost me hundreds of dollars a month combined. "What real difference could a short drug holiday make?" I'd argue with myself. When I confided this to a friend, she admitted one of her drugs costs $477 per month, so she'd skip a week at a time. Another friend told me that her father stretched his blood pressure meds by taking them only every other day instead of every day. It was a great little money-saver, until he died of a massive—and most likely preventable—heart attack.

"People often do a test, stopping their medications for a few weeks, and if they don't feel any different, they stay off them," Bruce Bender, codirector of the Center for Health Promotion at National Jewish Health, told *The New York Times*. "This is especially common for medications that treat 'silent' conditions like heart disease and high blood pressure. Although the consequences of ignoring medication may not show up right away, it can result in serious long-term harm."

I understood that, but I also thought I knew my body well enough to avoid any serious difficulties if I wanted to tamper with the dosage of my daily antidepressant. Like many people who take SSRIs (selective serotonin reuptake inhibitors, which include Prozac, Zoloft, and Lexapro), I'd begun to experience tough sexual side effects, which can wreak havoc in the bedroom. "It can affect desire, arousal, and orgasm," says Dr. David Hellerstein, a professor of clinical psychiatry at Columbia University Medical Center. I had enough issues in that department already, and I didn't need another.

So, without consulting my doctor, I cut my dose.

The only way I can describe what happened is this: Several days into my self-prescribed reduced dose, a trapdoor opened in my mind, and I fell into the darkest hole of depression. Sure, I'd previously read online that when medications like Lexapro are suddenly stopped, you can experience "very serious emotional and physical symptoms." But I never expected to have just about all of them: anxiety, agitation, panic, suicidal ideation, depression, irritability, anger, mania, and a series of bizarre sensations like brain zaps, pins and needles, ringing in the ears, and hypersensitivity to sound. And it never occurred to me that a mere reduction, not a full stop, would trigger this cascade of emotions and side effects.

I called my doctor, who told me to go back to my previous dosage—stat, or *right away*.

I now understand what drove me—and drives countless others—to nonadherence. Taking four or five pills every day reminds me of my chronic health conditions. When I look at myself in the bathroom mirror, I see a healthy and vigorous guy. When I open the medicine cabinet, however, I see someone who has heart disease, suffers from depression and anxiety, and often can't sleep. "Medications remind people that they're sick. Who wants to be sick?" a friend with heart disease says he told his doctor when asked why he wasn't following doctor's orders. And it's not like an antibiotic that you might take for seven or ten days; these medications are often for life.

Having witnessed firsthand what can happen when you play doctor in your own life, I now have a seven-day pill organizer to keep me on track. When I'm tempted to skip doses, I remember that I'd find myself face-to-face with the incriminating evidence—the pills I should have taken—the next time I open my organizer. At the very least, it's a reminder. So, too, is the stroke my dad nearly had when he lied to his doctor about taking his blood pressure meds.

Note to self: from here on out, I will remember that my doctors have something I don't—a medical degree—and that being honest with them is what's best for me in the long run (and makes it more likely that I will *have* a long run).

I Won't Refuse
to Change My Ways

"Nevertheless, she persisted" may be an inspiring motto in political circles, but insistence and resistance aren't always great qualities as we age. Learning to give a little, and dig out of certain well-worn ruts, can go a long way.

As TIME GOES BY, I'VE taken more and more comfort in certain routines, especially a Sunday-morning ritual that I've dubbed "walk, eat, flow." For many years, I started by taking my Jack Russell terrier for a walk by the river, eating a light breakfast, and then flowing through my asanas at a "mindful yoga" class. I didn't realize quite how rigid I'd become about my routine until a certain yoga class showed me that my routine had become not a well-worn path, but a rut.

This realization is likely why I laughed out loud when I read a National Institutes of Health study titled "My Parent Is So Stubborn." The authors might well have been describing mine. Older parents, the study authors wrote, respond to advice or help from their adult kids by "insisting, resisting, or persisting . . . commonly viewed as stubbornness."

Oh, and how stubborn Mom and Dad became as they grew older. My mother refused to take up her throw rugs even as my father repeatedly tripped and fell on them. ("I like how they look," she maintained.) After many falls, my father finally allowed a handyman to install grab bars in the shower, then called him back the very next day and had them removed. ("I don't like how they look.")

I don't want to become "insisting, resisting, or persisting" like my folks—although I sometimes fear I may be on my way. Which brings me back to my deepening rut. One Sunday, I showed up to yoga class to find Amy, my teacher, seated cross-legged at the opposite and darker side of the room from her usual place. "What's up with that?" I asked as I tried to orient myself to this new configuration. "You'll see," she said. I had not thought much about it before, but with Amy as my North Star in the room, I had known my place. With this change, I scrambled to figure out where to put down my mat.

As it turned out, this was a class on habits, which Amy defined as "ways that we have trained ourselves to act and react, so it's become almost automatic to act a certain way." She added later: "They are like ruts in our brains." The ruts only get deeper as we get older. "We usually think that change is bad," Amy continued, trying to convince a roomful of perplexed, gray-haired souls to get with the program. "I want us to try to see change simply as different. Without a value judgment."

Amy reminded us of the previous week's homework assignment: "Instead of brushing your teeth standing on two legs, stand on one. Stand on the other the next time. I want you to change it up and work on your balance."

But I *liked* my routines, my inner chatterbox prattled. I liked my "ruts," thank you very much. And I didn't like Amy shrouded in darkness against the back wall, or having to crank my head in the other—*wrong*—direction. Above all, I liked not having to think about where to sit. Very unmindfully in this mindful yoga class, I was used to just assuming my position.

As I thought about it, I realized that was true of much of my life. Although I am capable enough of switching up my habits, it's still hard to break free. For instance, several years ago I got lost while hiking through a fog bank, unable to find the full moon to direct me toward home. I knew our celestial neighbor was in the sky because I had seen it rise earlier, before disappearing into the fog. To find the moon again, I made a slow, 360-degree twirl, but I couldn't see anything other than thick mist. I got a little panicky. Still, I kept rotating. Again and again. Still lost. *Try. Fail. Repeat. Try. Fail. Repeat.*

Finally, I had a revelation. Years earlier, on a magazine assignment, this city boy had visited a "horse whisperer," who asked us to do one simple thing: get a horse to lift its hoof. "How hard could that be?" I asked myself. Well, I must have approached the horse a dozen times, sweet-talking, berating, bribing with treats, and finally trying to lift the goddamn hoof myself. No luck.

With my patience gone, the horse whisperer came over and said, "You need to figure out how to do this differently if you want to have a different result."

Finally, I understood, "I need to change my intent." I walked up to that horse like he belonged to me—and, damn it all, he lifted his hoof right up.

Lost in the fog, I recalled that lesson. "Hey, Steven, this is not working. You need to try something else." It was all I needed to snap out of my own fog, change course, and walk ten yards toward where I thought the Pacific Ocean (not a cliff) might be. The fog parted, and the moon winked. I was found. By being mindful—or let's just call it awake—I had discovered a new way to respond.

So simple. So radical.

Back in yoga class, Amy was adding to the confusion of the day by changing the flow. How much did I hate her now? She was throwing long-held traditions out the window: Left-to-right became right-to-left. Confusing! And not just for me. About two-thirds of my classmates were facing in the wrong direction by now. What a mess.

Still, the mess got me thinking: *I walk my terrier along the exact same route every morning. I shave my face in the same direction, from bottom to top, every day. I call my parents on Sunday afternoons.* I could have gone on . . . and on. I would call these my superficial habits, the ones that allowed me to move through the day without thinking much. Do this, followed by that. But this raised the question: Was I sleepwalking through my life?

When we got to the "fire log" pose, Amy went wild: "Reverse the placement of your legs and put your 'other' leg on top." I simply could not. My hips were, physically, too stubborn to change.

When the class ended, I breathed a deep sigh of relief. It had run long, there was a crick in my neck from looking in the "wrong" direction, and I was mentally exhausted from having had to pay attention to Amy's directives—instead of just going with the usual flow.

Still, I heard Amy as she reminded us, "With mindfulness, we can purposefully choose a new and different way to act."

I took her teaching to heart, starting the very next morning by walking my dog in the "wrong" or opposite direction (despite Zoe's insistent pulling to go the usual way). As I walked, feeling the morning sun on the other side of my face, I realized just about everything looked different. I noticed for the first time a beautiful pecan tree. A neighbor's swimming pool peeked through the hedgerow. Not to mention the sidewalk cracks and steps required new attention. In the meantime, Zoe found a new world to sniff—and to mark.

This all got me thinking about some of my more ingrained habits, those that help me glide through the day less mindfully, less in touch with myself and others. I default to reason before feeling; I withdraw from a problem instead of confronting it. *Try. Fail. Repeat. Try. Fail. Repeat.* Was there some of this I should revisit?

At the end of the class, Amy had given us a homework assignment. "When you wake up tomorrow, say one word to yourself: Gratitude."

The next day, as soon as my eyes opened, I reflexively reached for my iPhone, my brain buzzing with the day's to-do list. That little voice was already shouting out directives: "Do this, then that." Before my feet hit the ground, though, I remembered to say the word "gratitude." It interrupted all the noise, quieted me, and allowed me to focus. That small, simple word suspended the habitual way I usually started the day. No sleepwalking that day.

It won't be an easy promise to keep, but as I head into old age, I will stay flexible and not slide back into insisting, resisting, or persisting.

I Won't Tell My Life Story When Someone Asks, "How Are You?"

It's a rhetorical question—barely even a question at all! And nobody really wants to hear about stiff joints and indigestion—or worse—in response. I will remember the best answer to this question is almost always, "Fine, thanks, and you?"

"How's it going?" I heard a colleague casually ask of a fellow coworker in the break room. His reply: "Honestly, I'm so upset because I've just learned that my daughter's friend's younger sister has been diagnosed with cancer, although they say it's highly treatable, but it's so scary for a young woman ..." Whoa! Slow down. You lost me at "daughter's friend's...."

"How are you?" isn't actually a question, even if it masquerades as one. It's a greeting, a perfunctory call-and-response, pretty much like "hello." And the proper reply is generally a simple "Good, and you?" or "Fine, thanks!" At work, you might add a cheery "Glad it's

85

Friday!" but no more. Think about the "question" like this: When you say to your teenager or spouse, "Can you take the trash out, please?" you aren't really asking them to do it. The question mark is only there to be nice.

So when someone asks, "How are you?" think twice before answering honestly. Naturally, context matters. Consider whether you're speaking with a relative, friend, or colleague. Consider whether you're ill or not, how you're really feeling, and if that's information you want to share.

Here's a simple cheat sheet.

> FIRST: *Let's say you're actually sick in a serious or chronic way and someone you hardly know asks, "How are you?"* This just means "Hi," and does not imply—sorry—that the person is the least bit interested in your health. Your answer: "Good. And you?" Or, "I'm doing well. Thanks for asking." I will admit that in the months after my cancer diagnosis I often replied with too much detail. "I'm depressedangryandscared." I often went on . . . and on. When time was really short, I perfected my sublime and slimmed-down go-to answer: "Rotten." Many didn't know how to respond to my despair. I don't blame them. Bad, Steven. Too often, my lack of appropriate boundaries backfired because I found myself consoling those who had asked.
>
> NOW THIS: *You're ill, and a coworker (or someone not very close to you) already knows about your condition.* When they ask, "How *are* you?" their

emphasis implies they actually want to know more. Still, this is not an invitation to open the floodgates. Keep your reply to the point: "Getting along." Or "Better than I was." Even, "I have a scan next week . . ."

OR THIS SITUATION: *A friend or family member knows about your serious illness and is genuinely inquiring about your well-being.* The question is likely to be more specific, say, "How is your treatment going?" but also may be the garden-variety version, "How are you doing?" In these cases, authenticity matters. This is a time to answer honestly, giving as many or as few details as you're comfortable with and the situation allows. While we may not always be able to manage our illnesses, we can take control of how we talk about them, asserting our right to privacy—or disclosure—as we need.

When I was in the midst of my cancer treatment, I often found myself in a muddle and defaulted to this response: "I'm just not sure how to answer that today. But thank you for asking."

Finally, here are some pointers for those of us who have inquiring minds and genuinely want to ask a question that expresses concern. Basically we need better questions, like these: "How is your health these days?" "Have you been able to go back to work?" "Do you think you'll be able to take a vacation this year?" Each of them asks the same question, "How are you?" but allows those who are ill the option whether to go light or heavy.

The Covid-19 pandemic has also impacted what one writer for *The Atlantic* called "the mutual charade of 'I'm fine, thank you' . . . when both sides know that neither of them is fine." Better options include: "Are you still holding up okay?" "How are you coping?" Even, "What's your day been like so far?" Answers can be short ("I'm fine") or longer ("Well, it's been tough . . ."). The same writer also suggested, "the most important thing is to ask a genuine question that invites a genuine answer." Let's not pressure anyone to say they're okay when they're not.

The pandemic has also taught me that there's a distinction between our state of health and our state of mind. A fellow cancer survivor explained it to me: "I look at it this way. I could be in a lot of pain, have trouble walking, and be unable to see straight, and be miserable. Or I could be in a lot of pain, have trouble walking, and be unable to see straight, and be happy. I choose to be happy. I'm great, always great."

I'm going to choose to be great, too, even when I feel rotten.

I Won't Get My Knickers in a Twist at "Okay, Boomer"

Our generation has gotten more than our share of attention and indulgence over the decades. Rather than get prickly when a Gen Xer or Millennial plays this new insult card, I'll stop and think about it . . . and consider that maybe they're right.

I T STARTED WITH A BRIEF CLIP on TikTok, an online service most Boomers had never heard of. A split-screen video: On one side, our prototypical Baby Boomer—bearded, bespectacled, and baseball-capped. This white-haired guy is lecturing on the failings of Millennials and Gen Zers, with the usual litany of complaints. They're entitled, lazy, and self-absorbed, and they refuse to grow up. On the other side of the split screen, a young'un makes a placard that reads, "OK Boomer," held up repeatedly to counter each verbal volley.

Now, that little put-down has become the rallying cry of a generation (or two or three) fed up with the Boomers' condescension, greed, political corruption, and destruction of the planet. Ouch. But guilty as charged.

"The older generations grew up with a certain mindset, and we have a different perspective," nineteen-year-old Shannon O'Connor told *The New York Times*. O'Connor, who designed a T-shirt and hoodie emblazoned with the tagline "*ok boomer, have a terrible day*," added that "a lot of them don't believe in climate change, or don't believe people can get jobs with dyed hair, and a lot of them are stubborn in that view." According to O'Connor, when she uses "Okay, Boomer," it's like she wants to prove them wrong, that she will be successful, that the world is changing.

The snub has even made it to Dictionary.com, which calls it slang used "to call out or dismiss out-of-touch or close-minded opinions associated with the Baby Boomer generation and older people more generally." Or, more viscerally, *STFU, old people.*

Ageism wasn't far from the mind of a writer for *Inc.* magazine, a Gen Xer, who warned that casual or flippant use of "Okay, Boomer" could be a very serious and potentially expensive workplace issue. She continued: "You can't dismiss it as harmless banter," the author insisted, because it could create a hostile work environment and expose the company to a costly lawsuit. As George Takei, now eighty-four, would say, "Oh, *myyyy!*"

Frankly, this comeuppance seems like a small price to pay for our years of "hastening climate change, amassing national debt, raising college tuition, driving up real-estate prices, and electing Donald Trump," as a writer for *The Atlantic* summed it up. Step into some Millennial shoes, and we Boomers take on a villainous look indeed.

We Boomers have a long history of being unkind to Millennials. As these younger people struggle to pay off college debt and get started in adult life, we have mocked them as spoiled and entitled snowflakes and accused them of being avocado toast–eating freeloaders.

So yes, "Okay, Boomer" is meant to be nasty and dismissive. The younger generations are over us. But it's not mainly driven by ageism. In fact, anyone, regardless of age, can become a Boomer, because it's a state of mind. You just need the right—or wrong—attitude, said Jonathan Williams, a college student. "You don't like change, you don't understand new things, especially related to technology, you don't understand equality," he told *The Times*. "Being a boomer is just having that attitude, it can apply to whoever is bitter toward change."

The younger generations rightfully feel that we've left them an awful mess to clean up. They are right. Now what are we going to do about that, other than take offense?

I Won't Be Honest
to a Fault When
Lying Is Kinder

Sure, honesty is the best policy—and I've come to that conclusion more and more as I've gotten older. I make one exception: Lies may be a kinder and gentler way of talking to seniors who are not retaining information. Fibbing might be best for those in cognitive decline, and I will not insist on a perfect (and harsh) truth.

"AS CHILDREN, WE WERE TAUGHT to always tell the truth," the email began. "Now the father who taught us that has dementia. Now my brother wants to tell him small lies when he knows that dad will be upset by the truth. This is a conundrum for me that I'm not sure how to navigate. What should I do?" I paused as I read this question from one of my *Washington Post* readers. This one hit home, because I'd pondered the very same question during my own parents' illnesses.

Mom died in January 2017. Dad was in their bedroom when she passed, and he remained there while the undertakers, clad in black suits, came to the apartment and put her in a body bag to transport her to the funeral home. A week later, he spoke movingly at our mother's memorial service, engaging with the more than a hundred mourners who came to honor his wife of sixty-three years.

Two weeks later, the inquisition began:

"Steven, why isn't your mother in her bed?'

"What is your mother going to have for dinner tonight?"

"Where's Margot?"

Each time, I'd carefully remind him that Mom had died, and that she'd been cremated. "We're waiting for the spring thaw before we bury her," I added. No matter. He'd phone two, three, even five or six times a day with his same litany of questions, starting with, "Why isn't your mother in her bed?" Again and again I broke the news to him, and again and again he grieved. It was heartbreaking—and exasperating.

He hadn't exhibited any signs of memory loss or cognitive decline before then, and frankly, it happened only in conversations about our mom. Dad knew what day it was, that Donald Trump had taken office as president, and that my sister-in-law had a birthday coming up.

I wondered: How many times can you tell the truth and watch a loved one suffer the same loss again and again? Which is worse, telling a lie—or the harsh truth?

This terrible call-and-response clearly provided no solace or closure to Dad, and after speaking with a psychiatrist, I changed my approach. Instead of repeatedly telling the truth, I began what's known as "therapeutic fibbing," an effective yet controversial strategy. Basically, it's lying—or at least, not correcting a misconception—to decrease agitation and anxiety in a person with dementia.

Our conversations shifted:

"Steven, why isn't your mother in her bed?'

"Dad, she's in the living room watching television."

"What is your mother going to have for dinner tonight?"

"Mom's going to have what you're having."

"Where's Margot?"

"She's visiting neighbors in the apartment building."

Slowly, Dad's agitation decreased. So, too, did his near-constant interrogations. He died only three months after our mother—I hope thinking that he'd be joining Mom for dinner that night.

I learned I wasn't alone in taking this approach. About a year after my parents' deaths, I spoke with former Wisconsin governor Martin Schreiber, whose wife, Elaine, suffers from Alzheimer's. He's perhaps the best-known proponent of therapeutic fibbing. In a telephone interview, Schreiber, then seventy-nine, told me how he justifies this approach. "Elaine repeatedly asks, 'How are my parents?' Early on in her illness, I told her the cold truth, which is that both of them are dead. The shock on her face was so devastating, because she worried that she might not have gone to the funerals or said goodbye." Over time, Schreiber said, he could clearly see the anxiety that the truth provoked, which is why he started telling her, "Your parents are very, very happy. In fact, your mom is at church."

Schreiber said that there's no benefit in repeatedly trying to correct loved ones, and that a fib can actually draw the caregiver closer to the patient. "This is about the importance of joining the world of the person with Alzheimer's," he said with great compassion.

I understood.

Before we hung up, Schreiber relayed one last story. Not that many years ago, he said, Elaine had referred to her husband as "a turkey," and then told him matter-of-factly, "I'm beginning to love you more than my husband." Schreiber didn't bother to correct her, nor did he ask about her "turkey" of a husband. "I just grabbed that moment of joy," he said.

I wondered if there were limits to this approach and reached out to an expert for a better understanding of how far loved ones should go.

Jason Karlawish, codirector of the University of Pennsylvania Memory Center, cautioned that there's a big difference between accepting a patient's different sense of reality and mocking it, which he says he's witnessed all too often in more than twenty years of practice in this specialty. "You don't make eyes to people around you. You don't snicker. You don't joke that it's the 1960s when it's the 2020s."

So I will overcome my natural aversion to lying and be respectful of the "other" realties in which my loved ones live. It doesn't hurt anyone—and it helps them a lot—to join them briefly in their imagined world. I hope others will visit me, too, should I take a similar trip.

I Won't Worry About What I Can't Control

A friend once advised me to stop worrying about what might happen and focus on what's happening now. It's not easy to "wait to worry," but it was good advice at the time. I'll try to heed it as I get older and have even more to worry about.

IT WAS THE MIDDLE OF WINTER; the dry heat was blasting in my parents' New York City apartment. Dad's nose started to bleed, again, as it did most mornings. This time, before the health aide could intervene, he picked up his cell phone to call 911, telling the operator he had an "emergency." Within minutes the paramedics arrived, rushing him to the nearest ER, where he was turned away without treatment because a run-of-the-mill nosebleed isn't, well, an emergency.

It had been a long struggle. Ten springs earlier, Dad had consulted with no fewer than five neurologists, including the world-famous Oliver Sacks, because no one

could give him a definitive diagnosis for his neuromus-
cular degeneration. Soon after his appointment with Dr.
Sacks, Dad emailed me, his calm words belying a
growing panic: "I have some sort of degeneration in the
cerebellum, cause unknown, no treatment, no cure.
Thank God it's so slow moving." He then proceeded to list
a half dozen "what ifs"—"what if I can't talk, what if I can't
walk, what if your mother gets sick . . ."

I tried to get Dad to stay rooted in the here and now
and not obsess over all those "what ifs." I'd learned from
experience: "What if I have a recurrence?" "What if my
hair doesn't grow back?" That approach even extended
to the dating front: "What if he doesn't text me back?" My
personal mantra had become: "Wait to worry."

I wanted my philosophy to be his, too.

Dad's inclination toward premature worry was nothing new. Even before this malady, he'd always expected
the worst—whether it be financial or medical. I first understood this when it came to his own mother. For more
than sixty years, Grandma Marian had lived in a two-
story walk-up, where she enjoyed a lovely view of the
garden below. She reached her second-floor foyer via a
narrow flight of stairs, and my father worried that one
false wobble, and . . . well, you get the idea. From my dad's
perspective, this was a case of "when," not "if."

Actually, Grandma managed those ups and downs
quite capably, well into her mid-eighties, when my
father gave her an ultimatum. "Mother, you have to
move to the downstairs apartment," he told her. "Otherwise you'll become a prisoner at home." She refused. I
tried to help Dad imagine other scenarios, mostly rely-

ing on dark humor. "Perhaps she'll die suddenly of a heart attack," I suggested. "Or maybe she'll simply pass away in her sleep, in her own bed." The most likely scenario: Grandma would move to an assisted living facility.

So many possibilities, all impossible to predict.

Grandma rebuffed Dad every step of the way, not only navigating her own stairs but continuing her thrice-weekly subway trips from Queens to Manhattan to go to the theater and see her friends. Dad entreated me to join forces with him, which was when I first explained my "wait to worry" theory. My father—a left-brained academic—understood it intellectually, although he didn't accept it.

Honestly, the lesson hadn't come easily to me, either. Years earlier, as I was finishing chemotherapy, my previous worry ("Will I survive?") took a back seat to my new one ("Will I relapse?"). My oncologist did his best to alleviate my fear by reminding me that I had a good prognosis. He also threw out a free life lesson: "Although you can't control whether or not your cancer recurs, you can control how much you let the fear of recurrence affect your life."

Back then, I found that much easier said than done, as I (like my dad) tended to worry—a lot. Finally, a good friend asked me rhetorically, "Why spend the time worrying about what might happen when you can only control what's happening right now? I say throw it in the f*ckit bucket and have a glass of wine." I had no problem with the wine suggestion, but it was hard for me to let go of that fear.

I know it makes no sense, but I believed that by worrying, I could affect what happened. If I didn't worry
about the worst possible outcome, it would surely come
to pass.

At wit's end, I reached out to a friend of my mother
who had long been fighting her own cancer battle. I
dumped all my fears on Marion, especially my recurring
nightmare of relapsing. "It's all so out of my control," I
complained. When I was done, Marion—who'd been
through the wringer—was ready for me. She acknowledged my feelings but then dispensed that pithy piece of
advice: "Wait to worry."

I thought it was nonsense, and worry I did, constantly.
I self-medicated to escape my worst fears and refused to
shop in bulk. (Surely I would never eat that much mus-
tard before reaching my personal expiration date.) Then
one day I passed out, the result of a combination of too
much Scotch, marijuana, and prescription meds.

That's when Marion suggested I start practicing
guided imagery to calm myself. Three times a day for ten
or fifteen minutes, I lay on my sofa, closed my eyes, and
created a mental image of Pac-Man warriors devouring
my nasty cancer cells as I told myself, "My cancer cells
are weak and confused. I'm imagining them falling apart
like ground hamburger." I ended each session with "My
body is healthy and free of disease, and I'm reaching my
goals and fulfilling my life's purpose."

It took weeks, but I slowly regained a sense of self-
mastery, and with it a certain peace. I grew less afraid of
the what-ifs and stopped dwelling on them—and started
to enjoy the right-now again. I even found myself begin-

ning to accept Marion's advice. Yes, I could stay in the moment and "wait to worry."

Marion's mantra also paid off for her, big-time. Initially, she'd been given a life expectancy of six months, but she proved the doctors wrong by living eleven years from the day she'd been diagnosed with cancer. During those years, her two daughters and son got married, and she became a grandmother three times over. Her final years were spent joyfully in the moment, not mired in worried what-ifs.

Dad was never able to adopt my "wait to worry" mantra, which I discovered in, of all places, Grandma Marian's papers. Eight years before she passed away, my grandmother had written, "If can't change the situation, I must change my attitude for my own peace of mind."

That's my plan, too. I hope I won't follow Dad's worried path, but Grandma Marian's rosier one. Even if the destination is the same, I want to enjoy the garden views with joy, not fear.

I Won't Stop
Believing in Magic

Sure, it sounds kooky that a well-educated, rational man like me would put his faith in talismans. It's not that I don't believe in science, but there's a certain "Fairy God Bunny" who kept me alive in the past—and I won't give her up now. Or ever.

THE VELVETY RABBIT WITH BIG FLOPPY EARS and a silver tiara came to me with a name tag that read "Fairy God Bunny." That was when I was in my mid-twenties and had cancer. For five years, I carried this gender-bending rabbit with me everywhere, including to the hospital for labs, CT scans, and X-rays. I was never shy about introducing them to anyone, nor did I feel foolish, even though I was a twenty-six-year-old PhD candidate.

My friend Cynthia had given me the bunny soon after my testicular cancer diagnosis, reminding me several times that it had "magical powers." She later boosted those powers by adding a wand trimmed in gold lamé to complement its frilly tutu. That bunny was intended to be my talisman, a magical defender against my cancer.

Cynthia anticipated my skepticism. I'd grown up in an age of science, when facts and data reigned supreme. As a young boy I'd been a three-time visitor to the 1964 World's Fair, where I had a front row seat to a dizzying array of new technologies, including color TV, the picturephone (way before Skype or Zoom), and the promise of space travel. As a teen I excelled at Manhattan's Stuyvesant High School, famous for its geek curriculum.

When first diagnosed, I turned to science, reading every evidence-based, peer-reviewed study I could get my hands on. I hoped to make the best-informed treatment decisions. My odds of survival were actually pretty decent, but as an invincible twentysomething, I wasn't prepared to accept *any* chance of not making it to the ripe old age of thirty—or beyond. Put simply: I wanted to boost my odds of survival.

To do that, I had to become a kid again. Or maybe it's more accurate to say I chose to look at the world through the eyes of a child. For instance, growing up, I had a sense of wonder that knew no bounds. I believed in the miracle of Christmas, which in our family had nothing to do with Jesus. The tree, usually a Scotch pine, twinkled with red, blue, green, orange, and white lights, protecting us—as folklore tells us—against dark and evil spirits.

I believed in the unknown and the unknowable—even the impossible.

In time, I grew up, and became a "bah humbug" kind of fellow. I turned up my nose at the winter wonderland, especially when it came to Christmas "miracles." I came to detest the schmaltzy CD *A Christmas Miracle* featuring Donny Osmond, The Moody Blues, and—God help me— Barry Manilow. I could not bear *Miracle on 34th Street*, the tear-inducing story about Kris Kringle that introduced me (and the rest of the world) to Natalie Wood. "Argh," I used to say to all those "miraculous" stories of families reunited, kids' lives saved, and even suicides prevented— including the Jimmy Stewart classic *It's a Wonderful Life*.

Somewhere along the way I'd lost my sense of wonder.

Enter the bunny, exactly when I needed a strong dose of magic, if not wonder. My Fairy God Bunny would start me on a journey of trying to regain the magic.

Years later, I learned I wasn't alone in this quest. Stuart Vyse, a psychologist and the author of *Believing in Magic: The Psychology of Superstition*, told me that many people turn to "irrational beliefs" in times of dire need. Whenever medical science does not provide a cure, he said, there's going to be a "psychological gap, the need of something better." Thus we have superstition, magic, paranormal beliefs, and religion.

"It's not uncommon to be of two minds and to say, 'I know this is crazy, but I'll feel better if I do it anyway,'" Vyse said.

I never abandoned conventional medicine. I followed my oncologist's orders: Three surgeries. Four rounds of chemo. Years of follow-ups. But I would not leave my fate in doctors' hands alone. The Fairy God Bunny would be my amulet.

Actually, I learned if you look back far enough, before knowledge and reason overshadowed faith, talismans and amulets—proxies for magic—had their place in any self-respecting doctor's medicine bag. There is documented use of these objects, believed to have magical powers, that dates back at least to the medieval period, when they were an addition to—not replacement for—surgery.

The use of medical talismans has persisted. Dr. William Bartholome, a pediatrician and bioethicist at the University of Kansas Medical Center, wrote prolifically about his struggle with metastatic esophageal cancer—and his collection of forty frogs. "Bill's frogs were totems or talismans that he believed brought him luck," said Martha Montello, his friend and a lecturer at the Center for Bioethics at Harvard Medical School. Montello pointed out that her friend lived "an amazing five years" after diagnosis, much longer than his doctors had predicted. And that's the kind of magic I believe in.

Do I sound like a kook? I don't think so—but then, no kook ever does.

Ted Kaptchuk, a Harvard physician, told a *New Yorker* writer several years ago that he'd always "believed there is an important component of medicine that involves suggestion, ritual, and belief." He added, "All ideas that make scientists scream."

Kaptchuk is the chief of Harvard's program in placebo studies and the therapeutic encounter, which is focused on studying the power of the mind to influence health outcomes. In that same interview, he noted that medicine has known for centuries that some people respond to the power of suggestion—but not why or how.

About his tenure at Harvard, Kaptchuk wrote me in an email, "I haven't been twiddling my thumbs." He sent along a list of the more than a dozen studies he's either led or participated in that show how placebos, rituals, beliefs, and talismans play a role, albeit modest when compared with surgery and medication.

When you're in a fight for your life, "modest" is something to hang on to.

Five years after my diagnosis, my oncologist told me I was cured. I know I owe that cure to science and well-trained doctors. But I also think the hope embodied in the bunny made a difference to my well-being by reducing my anxiety, decreasing my heart rate, and improving my sleep, all of which gave me more good days than bad.

Can I prove it? No. Does that mean it's not true? No. As Kaptchuk told *The New Yorker*, "We need to stop pretending that it's all about molecular biology. Serious illnesses are affected by aesthetics, by art, and by the moral questions that are negotiated by practitioners and patients."

All ways of saying, by luck or magic. To paraphrase C. S. Lewis, I hope I'll never be too old to believe in fairy tales.

PART II

Stupid Things I Won't Do Tomorrow

We are always the same age on the inside.
—GERTRUDE STEIN

I Won't Blame the
Dog for My Leaky Pipes

*My dad wouldn't discuss anything about his worsening
bladder leakage, even after it was obvious to all of us. I
know the drips and drizzles are not fun topics, but I
promise I'll face them like any other physical changes
and take advantage of the many products that can help.
I will wear the goddamn Depends.*

LATE ONE NIGHT, I TEXTED my sister about Zoe, my
then-sixteen-year-old Jack Russell terrier: "The
dog is now on a sedative for dementia."

Julie replied, "That's good. Does it help her make it
through the night?"

Me: "Mostly. But it doesn't stop her from peeing. I'm
taking a pill, too."

Julie: "For the peeing or sleeping. Ha!"

Ha, indeed. Pee jokes—gotta love 'em (or at least take
them, from certain people, anyway), even when you don't
love the message. My family can find humor in (almost)
anything, and we have a long history of off-color humor.

Even as my siblings and I move into the golden years ourselves, age has not dampened our enthusiasm for a good sprinkle joke. At least, not yet.

I hope that doesn't change as we move into the target demographic for ads for pads. You can hardly watch the evening news (viewed primarily by Boomers) without landing smack dab in a copywriter's bulls-eye. How many ways can we address the issue of leaks and overactive bladders without mentioning the dreaded words "urinary incontinence"?

"Designed to fit your body and your life, improved core for better protection and comfort, so you can walk with poise and not worry about leaks. If sneezing or laughing causes bladder leaks, Always Discreet Moderate Pads offer protection." Or "Stay fresh and confident with Poise pads and liners. They're designed specifically for Light Bladder Leakage (LBL), making them an easy choice for the one in three women who experience LBL."

I learned an early lesson about leaks from my first dog, a cocker spaniel named Billic. In her later years, Billie suffered from "a little spritz," as Whoopi Goldberg described bladder leakage in her TV ads.

For Billie, the uncontrolled piddling and puddling started when she was about twelve. Early on, I'd scold her upon discovering another wet spot on the carpet—or worse, on the duvet cover. "Bad girl, bad girl!" I'd shout, full of judgment, and she'd run for cover, her tail hidden between her hind legs. In frustration, I put down "pee pads" all around the house, resenting the old pooch for staining and soiling the floors (and more). But that was before I realized my four-legged creature had a certifi-

able medical condition: age-related urinary incontinence. How can you shame anyone—even a dog—for
something they can't control?

The vet recommended Proin, a medication that's
highly effective at controlling leaky canine bladders, but
whose side effects can include seizures and strokes. I
didn't want to take those risks, so I told the vet "no,
thanks." And so, every morning began with a cup of joe
and a search mission for her nocturnal mishaps. Too
often, I found the puddles with my stocking feet.

Fortunately, humans have incontinence medications
with far fewer risks, which I wish I had known when my
dad started with his "drizzle." I also wish he'd known he
was among the thirty-seven million older Americans, or
one in five over forty, who suffer from a leaky bladder. On
some level, I believe that would have made a difference
to him. After all, who hasn't thought that they are unique
when it comes to what troubles us most? (I know I have.)

I have this tableau etched in my memory: I see Dad
reading on his chaise lounge, my dog curled tightly on
his lap. Soon she'd be snoring—and then my dad would
be, too. Our family loved seeing them together like that.
But as they both got older, there would be a telltale wet
spot visible on Dad's pants after Billie jumped off his lap.
He blamed it on Billie every time. Others were not so sure.

We tried to joke about it with my dad—after all,
humor is the best medicine—but he couldn't (or wouldn't)
laugh along with us. I understand now there was nothing
funny to be mined. This wasn't a faux pas like leaving a
price tag on a new sports coat or even forgetting to zip
up your fly. I regret not having shown more empathy for

what Dad was going through, and I think my efforts at humor reflected my own discomfort and fear. "Like the father, so goes the son" is an adage I've heard repeatedly in my life. I hoped not in this instance.

Over time, Billie's condition got worse, and she would sometimes wake up soaked in her own urine. I'd never seen a dog exhibit shame until then, when she would greet me with her head and tail down in humiliation. On those mornings I'd pick her up gently from her bed and take her to the tub for a soothing bath. There was no more "bad girl" talk. Instead, I gave her an abundance of treats—and accepted her leaky pipes as our new normal.

Dad, too, wet his bed with increasing regularity; his soiled sheets had to be removed and washed every day. Still, he refused to wear an adult diaper. I confess, at the time I felt more frustration than empathy. "Wear the goddamn pads!" I wanted to shout at him. "Don't make us change your sheets every morning." We remained locked in a tug-of-war—with no winner, only losers.

When it came to my mother, I was more successful—not with changing her behaviors, but with my reactions. One time, she got out of bed and walked to the dresser, pulling open the bottom drawer as if it were a toilet seat. Too late to stop her from urinating in the drawer, I voiced no exasperation, no plaintive and multisyllabic "Mooooom!" Instead, I steadied her, wanting only to prevent a fall.

Without missing a beat, the health aide helped Mom to the bathroom to clean up while I threw her sullied clothes into the hamper and wiped down the bureau. In a fresh nightgown, Mom got back into bed for a well-deserved night's sleep, surrounded not with shame, only love. I hope those close to me will show that kind of compassion if—when—I start to leak. And I pray that at least on this measure, the son won't be like the father because I'll be wearing my adult diaper.

I Won't Keep Driving When I Become a Threat to Others

My siblings and I battled with my mother for years about her driving. When we felt that she had become an actual threat, we did the unthinkable and turned her in to the state. I will never make anyone who loves me have to do that.

OR YEARS, I LISTENED to horror stories from friends about their elderly parents' adventures behind the wheel. "It starts out as mystery dents on the rear bumper," one began. "Somebody must have hit the car when it was in the parking lot," she quoted her father's explanation.

Soon, it amps up into mishaps and mayhem. Here's what others told me:

"My brother took away my mother's keys after she totaled her Camry in a parking lot. She couldn't move her foot off the gas."

"My father refused to stop driving even when he was so close to parked cars that he tore off multiple side-view mirrors—and denied that he had done so. My sister was visiting from out of state and made him go back around the block to see the damage."

Too often, it ends like this:

"There was an incident a few years ago when an elderly driver ran a red light, plowed right over the top of a blind person in a crosswalk, killing him, and then plowed into a telephone pole, killing himself. [This] is a nightmare that could happen to anybody if in the end they are too proud to give up their keys."

Then it became our family's turn.

On my mom's eightieth birthday, she bought herself a sporty, fire-engine-red Lexus that could go from zero to 60 miles per hour in 6.9 seconds. Her driving had been the subject of enormous worry among all family members for several years, but she loved high-octane cars, and she was not going to deny herself this shiny, fast, birthday present.

Picture it: an old lady with scoliosis, standing just under five foot two. She could barely see over the steering wheel of her prized new hot rod, but oh, how she loved putting that pedal to the metal.

Within a few months, though, I noticed a couple, then three, then four dents on the car. "What happened, Mom?" I'd ask casually, trying to keep judgment out of my voice. "I don't know," she'd reply noncommittally, although we both knew she knew more. At one point, my brother, riding shotgun to Mom, had to forcibly grab the steering wheel from her hands, giving it a sharp turn to the right to avoid a head-on collision. I, too, had been witness to hair-raising close encounters with cyclists and joggers.

At least we knew we weren't alone in our angst. A friend relayed this story:

"My husband's feisty eighty-eight-year-old grandmother in Florida occasionally drove her ancient car up the four-lane highway to the store, at slow times. When renewing her license, she failed the vision test. When the trooper told her he could not renew her license, she threw her keys at him, telling him to take the damn things and just how in the hell was she supposed to get home. She died peacefully in her recliner three weeks later, and I always believed the loss of her independence was the contributing factor."

Indeed, I was fully aware of just how much the car meant to Mom, both literally and as a metaphor for her independence. In practical terms, it was her means of transportation to the market, hairdresser, and her social bridge games. Even more than that, she loved being the lady with Jungle Red nails in the shiny red Lexus.

I couldn't help but think of the Beach Boys singing about how she'd have fun until her daddy took her T-bird away.

In her case, though, it would be her kids who took the red Lexus away.

After each new dent, we tried reasoning with her. "How about hiring taxis or Ubers?" we suggested, or asking Sheila, her health aide, to take her for visits and errands? When we suggested "the nuclear option"—giving up the keys—Mom flat-out refused.

Six months after buying the Lexus, she surprised us one day by arriving home in a smaller, less tricked-out model (still red, of course). That first car had had "a design flaw," she told us, beaming. A quick call to the dealer confirmed that there had been no flaws in the first car. The newer car, the dealer explained, did have fewer bells and whistles, fewer distractions.

Mom was ebullient. "This car will make it easy for me to drive again," she declared. The rest of us were hopeful but far from convinced.

After more fender benders, Mom became convinced the problem was her eyes, so she had cataract surgery. That resulted in better vision, but no discernable improvement in her driving ability.

Finally, we staged an intervention: We sat down together as a family to beg her to stop driving. She listened intently, making eye contact with each of us as we spoke in turn. When we had finished, she paused for a moment and then said bluntly, "Thank you very much for your concern. Now you can go f*ck yourselves."

At that point, my sister, a lawyer, upped our parents' umbrella insurance policy. We talked frequently among ourselves, concerned that Mom's fender benders would inevitably lead to more serious accidents. How would we live with ourselves if she maimed—or even killed—someone? How could we stop this before she became a deadly threat on the road?

Other elders I knew acted more responsibly. One wrote me:

"After sixty-seven years of driving without a chargeable accident, I hit a telephone pole (at 1 mile per hour) and the very next day drove across a sidewalk. That was the last time I drove, realizing that the next time could be the end of me or someone else. Now I have to rely on others, face occasional cabin fever by being housebound and frustration about my lack of mobility. That's the downside. The upside—many of my friends have followed my example, keeping the roads safer and preserving family harmony. Seniors, take note."

Finally, one day, Mom backed the Lexus out of the driveway right into a neighbor's legally parked car. (She'd stopped using the mirrors and couldn't turn her neck sufficiently to see behind her.) Mom took no responsibility for the damage inflicted, even going so far as to blame our neighbor for parking in *her* way. We were horrified to see her so easily justify this behavior (and without her knowledge, we paid for the damage to the neighbor's car).

With the stakes rising, my siblings and I talked about taking away her keys. But we feared Mom would call a taxi to take her right back down to the dealership, and she would return with another set of keys—or another car. We did some digging and discovered that in New York State, where my parents lived, anyone can file an anonymous "request for driver review." The form asked for some basic information before getting to the heart of the matter: "Your reasons for reporting this driver."

We continued to debate whether to file the form, believing that it would surely result in the revocation of her driving privileges. But we also know she'd be devastated, betrayed, and insulted. How would I feel if the tables were turned and someone did this to me? Outraged, for starters.

But how would I feel if one of my loved ones were hit by an elderly driver whose children had had this same debate but did nothing? What if Mom hurt or killed someone? That was unthinkable. Together we decided: It was time to turn her in.

As the eldest, I was designated to sign, seal, and deliver the form to the DMV; my brother and sister added their names as "others who agree with your assessment of this driver." And we made a pact never to disclose our role in this whole mess—at least, not while Mom was alive.

It took a few months, but Mom eventually received a letter from the DMV informing her that she had been reported. She was summoned to take both written and road tests within thirty days. Talk about livid. To the day she died, she remained convinced that it was her neighbor—the one whose car she'd hit—who had ratted her out. Her outrage masked equal parts humiliation (she thought she was a great driver) and fear (she couldn't bear the thought of losing her independence). Right about then, she was diagnosed with lung cancer and scheduled for surgery. In this, she found a silver lining: Her illness gave her a thirty-day extension for taking the two exams.

While recovering from her surgery, Mom, determined as ever, enrolled in a local driving school. She knew the stakes were high. The DMV letter made it clear that if she failed to appear or to pass, her license would be revoked. "I've been driving my entire lifetime," she explained to me. "I'll know when it's time for me to stop."

On the appointed day, Mom's health aide drove her to the DMV, where she passed the written exam but failed the road test. When I talked to her later in the day, she sounded dejected but also furious at the examiner, whom she claimed had been rude and condescending. A week later, his evaluation arrived in the mail: He had dinged Mom for poor judgment, being inattentive to traffic, failing to stay in the proper lane, impeding traffic flow, poor acceleration, poor steering, delayed braking, and more. His final admonishment: "Extremely dangerous!! Turns wide into wrong side of road! Poor late braking. No observation at all backing. Completely unaware of surroundings. FAILED."

Just as Mom had alleged, the examiner's comments were rude and condescending. They were also entirely accurate. Mom's license was revoked, and she was issued a nondriving New York State ID card instead.

For my siblings and me, our mission was accomplished. We did our best to ferry her to and fro, as did her aide and some neighbors. But her world grew considerably smaller, shrinking week by week as both her disease and old age took their toll. I remained conflicted about what we—what I—had done. But I had not a single regret about the results.

After Mom died, I found among her papers a Ziploc bag that contained all the correspondence with the state about her driver's review. It was as though she had packed it up for me, a message in a bottle for a day yet to come. I'm keeping it close, for the inevitable time when I need to turn in my keys. Will I be self-aware enough to do so voluntarily? I hope so. Not too long ago, I pulled out of my driveway, nearly backing into a neighbor's parked car across the street. I'd been in a rush and hadn't used my mirrors. Disaster averted, and I was very glad no one else had seen me. But in that moment, I knew what my mother must have felt like as she started having close calls. I also know all too well that this is a one-way street.

I Won't Stop
Enjoying Myself
(and Yes, I'll Have the
Occasional Candy Bar)

I'll live longer, with a better quality of life, if I eat well, but that doesn't mean I shouldn't enjoy a bucket of KFC and a candy bar once in a while. I hope to have a few indulgent friends or family members to join me and not judge me.

AS A CANCER SURVIVOR, a journalist, and a cardiac patient, I've thought and written an awful lot about nutrition and longevity over the years. I eat a (fanatically) healthy diet, don't smoke (cigarettes), and try to limit my Manhattans (which I prefer straight up and not too sweet). I hit the gym regularly, and I walk my dog three miles a day.

I'm also a confirmed chocoholic, and for years I believed—thanks to many published studies and accompanying news stories—that dark chocolate had health benefits: lowering the risk of certain cancers, decreasing blood pressure, and reducing the risks of diabetes, stroke, and heart disease. I had even read that dark chocolate counts—along with nuts, avocados, and blueberries—as a "superfood." What could be better than that—something I crave that also helps me live a healthier, longer life?

As a journalist, however, I know better than to believe everything I read, especially if it's melting in my mouth. So I decided to look past the consumer-oriented articles and dig deeper into the studies themselves. To help me sort it out, I called on Marion Nestle, the much-respected professor of food and nutrition studies at New York University, who has extensively studied the chocolate industry (most recently in her book *Unsavory Truth: How Food Companies Skew the Science of What We Eat*).

Nestle (no relation to the candy maker) told me right off the bat that it's not chocolate itself, but the flavanols in it that might have potential benefits. Ah, those messy details. Yes, flavanols are abundant in cocoa beans, which yield cocoa powder, which is then used to make chocolate. What the flashy headlines don't tell you, she noted, is that the amount of flavanols in a chocolate bar is not nearly enough to provide any kind of health benefit.

So since my one little square of dark chocolate is pretty skimpy on the flavanols—I should just eat more, right?

Not so fast. Nestle told me that if I were to eat more chocolate to increase my flavanol intake, I'd be consuming a lot more sugar, fat, and calories as well—bad, bad, and bad for my health and waistline. In fact, I'd have to chow down at least seven regular-size candy bars a day to get anywhere near the flavanols to make a positive difference. Even this chocolate lover has to admit that that's too much.

Despite all the marketing claims, chocolate is no match for kale in the health-food department.

I've also read that once you're past a certain age—seventy-five years, according to a Penn State study—eating well doesn't necessarily translate into aging well. Yes, you read that correctly, with the study's docs saying the message is, "Call off the dogs." Now we can add a more liberal diet to our other senior perks—like openly speaking our minds, being forgiven for being forgetful, and receiving discounts on almost everything.

To that very point, my friend Janet, who is in her fifties, emailed me: "I took my seventy-seven-year-old aunt out for lunch today. She has about six teeth, sits in wheelchair, and has a long list of ailments. She's also losing her memory a little bit. But when I asked her what she wanted to eat, she said chicken from KFC. It's not where I would go normally. But when I go out with her, I take her wherever she wants. She enjoyed every bite. And right now, she's probably eating the Baby Ruth candy bar we got for dessert from the dollar store."

I'm with Janet—and her aunt. I'll enjoy my dark chocolate when I can, and if the day ever comes that I need someone to push my wheelchair across the street to get some, I'll be very grateful if they accommodate me. I kind of hope it's a chocolate shop over there instead of a dollar store, but as long as it sells chocolate, I'll be happy.

I Won't Hoard
the Butter Pats

Or sugar packets from restaurants, or even the very nicest of cardboard boxes. If I can reuse or recycle something I will, but the time for collecting (or stockpiling) is over; at some point, it's time to declutter. I won't make my nieces—or a tag sale specialist—bulldoze through useless stuff in my attic, basement, every closet, and even the fridge.

AFTER MY PARENTS DIED, I could have opened a greasy spoon called Smucker's Café that served only grape jelly, strawberry jam, and their signature orange marmalade. That's how many of the little "portion cups" my parents had swiped from diners, along with free butter pats. Alas, there was more.

My parents died with not one but *two* houses to be emptied, doubling the heavy lifting for my siblings and me. We quickly discovered that rather than spending their final years decluttering, they'd actually been adding to a lifetime's worth of stuff. Mom and Dad had left us not only their own possessions, but a wall of file boxes containing letters, newspaper clippings, and photos from my father's mom (my pack-rat librarian grandmother). These boxes had not even been touched since Granny's death a quarter century before, when we'd spent weeks emptying her house.

I flashed back to that earlier cleanout. Deviating not one iota from his characteristic hyperefficiency, my father had set the ground rules before we arrived at our grandmother's house: "Everything's got to go from Marian's house. *Today.*" I can recall Dad handing me an oversized box with these words, "Do something with this, *now.*" What we did with them, I realized now, was defer the inevitable. Here they were again, patiently waiting for us to make that final call.

My sister, brother, and I debated whether to open Granny's boxes. "What secrets might we find?" I wondered. Confronted with the reality of how much time that could take, I suddenly became my father, barking to my siblings and their spouses: "Do something with this, *now.*" I decided that my grandmother's secrets were hers and hers alone.

Since then, I've been haunted by what we might have found inside those boxes, if only we'd made the time to look. I remember one banker's box I'd found in Granny's basement (labeled "Steven" in her old-fashioned script) that I had taken home when we cleaned out her house all those years ago. It took me more than a year to open it, and when I did, I was stunned to find my teenage journals inside. As I read them, I wrote in a new notebook, "The journals secretly harbored the record of my anxieties, panic attacks, and nascent depression when I was incapable of giving them any other voice. Without Granny, I honestly believe I would have become permanently lost to myself."

There was no time for such ruminations the day we cleared out the first of my parents' homes. We had a monumental task before us—a monument that added up to nearly 4,000 pounds carted off by my brother in his flatbed truck to the town's waste management facility. We created four stacks: one each for my brother, sister, and me, and the fourth for the dump. Any time my brother or sister started to wander down memory lane (*Do you remember when . . .*), I'd cut off the chat and shout, doing my best Dad impersonation, "Love it or leave it!"

When all was said and done, the dismantling of my parents' lives led me to become a devotee of *döstädning,* which translates to "Swedish death cleaning." Margareta Magnusson, the author of *The Gentle Art of Swedish Death Cleaning: How to Free Yourself and Your Family from a Lifetime of Clutter*, explains the simple yet brilliant approach: "It means you remove unnecessary things and make your home nice and orderly when you think the time is coming closer for you to leave the planet." Magnusson, who claims to be "somewhere between 80 and 100," urges her readers to start sooner rather than later to spare loved ones the odious and time-consuming chore. It's a version of Marie Kondo's "delight test" from her bestselling book, *The Life-Changing Magic of Tidying Up*. "[W]hen we really delve into the reasons for why we can't let something go," Kondo writes, "there are only two: an attachment to the past or a fear for the future."

As we finished clearing out my parents' beach house and city apartment, I had another flashback to the mid-1990s when my then-partner Barry and I emptied his childhood home after his dad died from colon cancer. The brick ranch had a neat, trim exterior, but inside, oh my God, this was a hoarder's palace. The front door opened onto mountains of newspapers and magazines, all piled so high that we had to navigate through narrow canyons to travel from room to room.

Once in the kitchen, we opened the fridge to find a stockpile of butter pats (foreshadowing what I'd one day find in my parents' refrigerator) and salad dressing containers. But the real shocker came once we entered the bathroom: Barry's father had painstakingly cleaned, dried, and repackaged hundreds of his used colostomy bags. I'm sure he didn't love them, nor could they have passed the "delight test," but he still couldn't leave them.

Back to my parents.

Once we'd finished their dejunking, I sat down with *Swedish Death Cleaning*, naturally a trim and slim volume, taking notes and creating a list of to-dos.

> *Visit [your] storage areas and start pulling out what's there. . . . Who do you think will take care of all that when you are no longer here?*

I started by throwing out two decades of tax returns, including all the supporting documents. Box after box. I then used those same boxes to crate my personal papers and book research, which I donated to my college library.

Life will become more pleasant and comfortable if
we get rid of some of the abundance.

I went through my dresser, packing up dozens of items that I hadn't laid eyes on in years, or that had out-lived their useful life, for the thrift shop.

It is a delight to go through things and remember
their worth.

One unexpected benefit of decluttering and death cleaning is the sweetness of revisiting the past. I still have shoeboxes of prints—thousands—taken from the 1960s onward, each box unhelpfully labeled "Photo-graphs." I am winnowing my way through them, one box at a time, looking for keepers. Sometimes I find joy in the discovered memories; at other times they weigh heavily. "Will I ever finish?" I wonder.

So I promise I won't leave my house filled with bric-a-brac, piles of letters, or mountains of clothes to be sorted through and then taken by relatives, donated, or trashed. I look around and echo my dad when I tell myself, "Do something with this, *now.*"

I Won't Wait
Until I'm Deaf to Get a
Hearing Aid (or, "What?
What Did You Say?")

Why do we accept reading glasses as necessary evils but treat hearing aids like signs of impending senility? They are smaller and less conspicuous than ever, and I will get mine if and when I need them. I won't suffer the isolation that comes with living in silence.

A T FORTY-FIVE, I NEEDED reading glasses. I got them. At fifty-two, distance lenses. Ditto. By fifty-six I had graduated to progressives, and all I remember thinking was "wow, these are expensive." Not once did I balk at getting spectacles as my vision started to deteriorate.

If and when I need hearing aids, well, that's another matter. Jennifer Finney Boylan, a professor at Barnard College and an opinion writer for *The New York Times*, summed up the quandary in a column: "Why, I wonder, is it that devices to keep you from being blind are celebrated as fashion, but devices to keep you from being deaf are embarrassing and uncool? Why is it that the biggest compliment someone can give you about your hearing aids is "I can hardly see them"?

Hear, hear! Professor Boylan.

I think my hearing is pretty good, but I haven't had it tested in . . . well, ever. Still, I am aware that I favor certain restaurants nowadays, which I freely admit has more to do with decibel level than Michelin stars. And I love that there's now a "Yelp for noise" that helps you find the quietest bars and restaurants in your city.

Friends with hearing loss have lots of advice when it comes to eating out. "To hear better, sit facing a wall rather than facing out." Another suggests I "pass up a table in favor of a booth because their fabric cushions and high back can create a little bubble of relative quiet in the middle of the racket." Finally, this: "Choose a table farthest away from the kitchen, especially if it's an open-concept restaurant."

I'm realizing some of their suggestions may be helpful to me, too, as a thought runs through my brain: "I wonder if my hearing isn't what it used to be. I wonder if I should get it checked out."

We have so many reasons not to use hearing aids: They're uncomfortable. They're ugly. They whistle. They hurt. They don't work in a large crowd. They're expensive. Above all, as Boylan wrote, "I thought it would make me seem old and undesirable." Or as a friend, who bought his first pair at age fifty, explained: "Yes, I felt that [the devices] would carry a stigma. But I was starting to feel the opposite stigma, of the person who had to keep asking others to repeat themselves, or sometimes completely missed conversations and fell out of it." That resonated with me.

For the last chapter of my father's life, he'd often shout at me, "Up your audio!" No one in our family—or his world—was spared this corrective. For Dad, a former television producer, this command meant we weren't speaking loudly enough. (Back in the day, I'd be in the control room with Dad and he'd bark the same phrase at his anchors.) If he were to be believed, his wife, three adult kids, and their spouses were monotonic mumblers. It was us, not him. To be heard, we had to shout.

I know Dad hated the idea of using a hearing aid, because he told me so. He also pointed out that the "beige banana boat" worn by his mother—our grandmother—marked a person as (as he put it) "deaf, daffy, and old." Grandma was none of those things, staying on the job as a librarian until well in her seventies and frequently going to the theater in New York City as an octogenarian. But she did wear a hearing aid that looked like a mutant insect resting behind her ear.

Even when I explained to Dad that the newest digital hearing devices are practically invisible (like the Mini-Behind-the-Ear-Hearing-Aid and the Completely-in-the-Canal versions), he still would not listen. Or perhaps he just didn't hear me.

Dad wasn't alone. More than forty-eight million Americans suffer from hearing loss, with one third of those sixty-five to seventy-four and half of those seventy-five and older needing—but not using—a hearing aid, according to the National Institute on Deafness and Other Communication Disorders. Denial is one barrier—

cost, another. The price of one hearing aid can range from fifteen hundred to a few thousand dollars—pricey!—depending on its style and features, according to the Mayo Clinic.

Thrifty is one word I'd have used to describe my grandmother. Despite the cost, she realized she needed to buy a pair, and I remember the exact day she made her decision. In fact, it registered as such a momentous experience that I wrote an entire journal entry about it.

As she often did, Grandma, then seventy-two years old, had taken me to the theater for a matinee—in this case, a production of *Bent*, the Tony Award–winning play about the persecution of gays in Nazi Germany. It starred a young, breathtakingly beautiful Richard Gere. Because nothing was too good for her "number one grandson," as she constantly referred to me, and because she knew she had trouble hearing, we had front-row seats.

Unfortunately, the theater didn't have any of the "assisted listening devices" for those who might have needed them, which meant Granny had trouble hearing the dialogue. She started nudging me, whispering to me in the way that those with hearing loss often do: loudly. "What did he say?" In a hushed voice, I'd fill her in. This worked reasonably well until the characters Max and Horst, imprisoned in a Nazi concentration camp for the crime of homosexuality, stood center stage in front of us. Literally three feet from Grandma and me.

Separated by an imaginary barbed-wire fence, the two men, their prison uniforms adorned with pink triangles to mark them as gay, began to make explicit (and, believe me, detailed) *verbal* love to each other. I was twenty-three, but I'd never witnessed—or heard—anything as sexually explosive as this scene. In a rhythm they moved to the climax: "Feel me." "It's so hot." "I'm kissing your chest." "Yes." "Hard." "Down." "Yes." "Down." And more. . . .

At each turn, Grandma elbowed me and asked, not *sotto voce*: "What are they saying?" "*What are they saying?*" "WHAT ARE THEY SAYING?"

"Shhh! I'll tell you later, Grandma!"

After the final curtain came down, I did tell her. The next time we went to a show, she was sporting her banana boats.

Lesson learned for Grandma.

My friend Daniel, in his early sixties, learned his lesson, too—and got his hearing aids—after his wife, Laura, told him point-blank: "You don't hear me and you check out a lot when you can't hear." He must have heard her, because he told me this on the phone one day after deciding to get a pair of hearing aids.

Once he started using them, Daniel described "a remarkable change." He could hear the birds, leaves, and the cicadas. "Even Laura!" He then understood that "the things you miss are missed. Sometimes you can tell that somebody has said something to you, which you don't quite understand, but in many cases, you don't even know that you're missing anything."

With any luck, I won't lose my hearing like my father and grandmother did (although the gene pool isn't looking good). If I do, I'll purchase the audio boost I need—preferably a Bluetooth-enabled model that can also stream music and podcasts. I'm keenly aware that not being able to hear what's going on around me shouts "I'm old" way more than sporting a hearing device does.

I've made my appointment with an audiologist—actually, with Daniel's. I'll let you know what I hear.

I Won't Fall Prey to Scams, Schemes, or Sleazeballs

Con artists deliberately target older people, knowing they are more easily confused, and duped, than younger ones. I will keep my guard up and remember that if something sounds too good to be true, it is too good to be true.

THE EMAIL CLAIMS TO BE from one of your grandchildren, or from someone who's with them. "I'm in Canada and I'm trying to get home but my car broke down and I need money right away to get it fixed" is one that came my way. Other pleas claim a relative has been mugged or in an accident, or needs money for bail. Regardless of the details, there's always an emergency—and the urgent need for you to wire money right away to help them out. And, of course, you do— why wouldn't you?

There's a very good reason not to. Chances are this is a scam, designed to fool you into parting with your cash, and it's surprisingly common. It's called the "grandparent scam," and it plays out again and again, year after year, snagging vulnerable seniors in its net.

This scam is designed specifically for older folks, although there are plenty of other schemes created with us in mind. There's the email that tells you that one of your bank accounts needs updating, just click here to get started, and before you know it, you've entered all your PII (personally identifying information), like driver's license, Social Security, and phone numbers; mother's maiden name; and so on.

Or you may be told that your visit to a porn site has been monitored (even if you don't watch "art movies"). One such scam claims, "while you were watching the video your web browser acted as RDP (remote desktop) and a keylogger provided me access to your display screen and webcam. Right after that, my software gathered all your contacts from your Messenger, Facebook account, and email account." What's more, the email alleges you were recorded viewing the grainy footage. ("Yep! It's you doing nasty things!" reads the text.) And if that weren't enough, the email claims all of your personal contacts—family, friends, coworkers—have been stolen. Now the blackmailer is giving you twenty-four hours to make a payment, often several thousand dollars. Pay up or risk exposure. (Even the innocent may be guilt-tripped into making a payment.)

Scammers know that older folks are especially easy targets for all sorts of schemes, including those involving credit cards, sweepstakes, charities, health products, magazines, home improvements, and affairs of the heart.

Many of us are lonely, willing to listen, and may be more gullible than younger people.

Take the example of a seventy-nine-year-old man who began telling his daughter about a woman he had met online; he was sending her money frequently. Although they'd never met, she professed her love through email, asking him to help buy food for her and her young son. How could he refuse? The daughter felt something was amiss, but her dad would not listen and continued to send money. Over the course of two years, he sent this stranger more than $700,000, nearly all of his life savings. The daughter eventually discovered the extent of the fraud when she received power of attorney over her dad's accounts.

Alas, this is not uncommon, according to the Stanford Center on Longevity and the Financial Industry Regulatory Authority's Investor Education Foundation. Those over sixty-five are more likely to have lost money to a financial scam than someone in their forties.

I saw this up close with my own mother—and it was long before she had dementia. While visiting for lunch one afternoon, I saw a package from a personal investment company on the dining room table. Knowing that Mom already had a financial advisor, I asked her about the new material. "Oh, he called me and asked if I was interested in getting a greater return on my investments," she replied airily, "and I said, 'sure!'"

She admitted that they'd spoken "many times." Mom loved the attention and the promises he made. Who wouldn't? After I found his business card, I emailed the guy a few times to let him know that Mom already had a financial planner and wasn't looking for anyone new. He made no response to me, but he persisted with Mom and set up an appointment to come to the house.

To the house! By this time, I had his number—literally and figuratively—and called him. "Leave our mother alone or else," I threatened. That was the last Mom heard from him, but I knew she wasn't his last potential victim. (A decade or so later, I actually received the identical solicitation from the same investment firm, with the same promises.) Frankly, I was a little surprised by how quickly I moved from being the protective son to being the potential victim myself.

Back in the dating market for the first time in nearly two decades, I've had some catching up to do. I'm talking about all those dating apps: Tinder, Match, OkCupid, and Grindr. It's a whole new world, fraught with new opportunities for love and heartbreak, catfishing and scams.

Soon after I signed up, I began to receive messages from what I'd call perfect boyfriend candidates with well-appointed apartments, excellent jobs, and, yes, model good looks. But as I learned, none too soon, many of them were fakes. The practice is known as "catfishing," which Urban Dictionary defines as a "fake or stolen online identity created or used for the purposes of beginning a deceptive relationship."

Let me tell you about "David" and me. Over a span of two years, David swiped right on my profile a number of times, which meant he "liked" me. His photo showed a muscular physique and a kind smile; he claimed to be forty-eight years old, six foot one, and 180 pounds. He wrote that he was an army "sargent," and while I don't expect perfection from anyone, I do think my dream man should know how to spell his job title: sergeant. In his profile, David had written one incoherent run-on sentence that began, "I want to met [sic] a man that has a good tolerance level and how far he can go in life," and ended with the hashtags, #LTR #lovingcare #soulmate.

The first time I came upon his profile I made an allowance for his spelling errors and poor syntax, swiping right myself. More recently, when he reached out—for perhaps the tenth time—I'd grown curious and played along. Very quickly in that exchange, David queried, "Would you commit to a relationship even if your soulmate was an army guy?" With no hesitation, I replied, "Absolutely. Are you in the Army?"

"Yes my handsome, how about you?" he shot back, using his telltale term of endearment and explaining that he was currently stationed in Afghanistan.

"Of course you are," I said to myself.

David quickly moved to take us off the app, a no-no if you want to protect your identity. "Can you kindly give me your Google hangouts so we can text, share pics, stay in touch and know more about each other?" he messaged. I knew better than that, sending him a Google Voice number, which cannot be used to decipher your identity.

A minute later, a text appeared from an untraceable number. "Hi my handsome. This is David." He explained he'd be back in the U.S. in a few months, seeking his "soulmate." Abruptly, he texted: "What's your full name and age?" He told me his name and that he was forty-eight. "Send me your pic, handsome."

I Googled his name and actually found a Twitter account with that exact name, with the same photos I'd seen on the app. His profile read, "I'm proud of myself in being honest and most trustworthy, I seek that in a mate, someone who is compassionate yet understanding who has a calm great personality." Instead of sending him any more photos, I texted, "Ok, I'll be back later!" and then blocked his profile and his phone number. A month later, David, ever persistent, messaged me from a new account: "How are you my handsome?" This time I reported him as a scammer and swiped left. Done.

(Much later, I came to understand that catfishing is big business in the online dating game. Perhaps those photos actually belonged to a real person, whose identity had been stolen.)

So I will follow the rules of "buyer beware." If it seems too good to be true, it's too good to be true. If I get a text or email that directs me to click here, I won't! And I'll never, ever, send money to anyone without verifying the story first. And when was the last time your children or grandchildren *emailed* you? Now, if they send a text message asking for help—well then, that's another story.

I Won't Burden
My Family with
Taking Care of Me

*Aging in place is the dream plan for a lot of us, but for
our families it can be more of a nightmare. I will make
the appropriate arrangements for my care, and not just
hope it all works out.*

As soon as my parents became eligible for Medicare,
my siblings and I started nudging them about planning for their future. They were healthy at the time, but we
found ourselves looking at their house with a concerned
eye. It had lots of steps, narrow doorframes, and uneven
floors, and it was a hundred miles from my sister, the nearest of us. We could easily imagine a nightmare unfolding.

What if one or both of them became disabled or seriously ill? What if one died first, leaving the other? My
brother Jay looked at continuing care communities
(where residents live independently until they need assisted living or skilled nursing care) near his Westport,

Connecticut, home. One such place looked excep-
tionally promising, albeit expensive. Its website waxed
positively poetic, highlighting its "charming boutiques"
and "challenging golf courses," and even its top-dog pet
sitting services.

Jay took my parents on the tour, which lived up to
many of its promises. He reported back to my sister and
me that all units, no matter their size, boasted private ter-
races or patios, oversized bedrooms and living areas, and
so much more. In the "fine dining" restaurant, a sample
dinner included tiger shrimp arancini, a choice of beef
tenderloin or sake tamarind-infused Chilean sea bass as
the entrée, and Kahlua crème caramel served with black-
berry compote for dessert, which is hardly how my
meat-and-potatoes parents usually ate.

"I hate fish," Mom reminded my brother as her way of
vetoing the idea.

Dad added his two cents, declaring, "Never. We will
age in place." And that ended the conversation, even
though both our parents continued to say to us for years,
"We don't want to become a burden to you children."

In time, it turned out that we "children" were the more
realistic ones. Dad did become disabled. Mom was diagnosed with lung cancer. And they did become a burden.
A generous long-term-care policy covered a great deal of
the in-home services they needed, but their living situation became the predicted nightmare. When a blizzard
isolated them for days without power, it was the first
time I truly heard fear in my dad's voice when he called
the local police. "I'm eighty years old. You need to plow
the road to us if we need to call 911."

In our parents' final years—at home—the three of us managed their finances, hired and fired health aides, called 911 when necessary (and tried to prevent emergency calls when not), and dealt with crises that had become routine. We took turns being "on-call," which meant sharing the duty to field emergency calls in the middle of the night. In every way, this caretaking proved exhausting, even as we kept hearing, "We don't want to become a burden."

After my parents died, and as I turned sixty, I vowed to do things differently. According to AARP, people turning sixty-five these days will probably live another twenty years, and 70 percent will need some level of long-term care. I needed a plan—actually, a revised plan, because until then I'd expected my husband to be a big part of my plan. But we had divorced. And so, with no guarantee that I'd find another partner and—like many LGBTQ people—with no kids, I had to think about an aging plan for just me.

Since my contemporaries are now approaching (or passing) Medicare age, I asked for their thoughts on senior living. A former work colleague told me, "Denial, Steven. Sheer denial." A high school friend hit the nail on the proverbial head: "Call me Peter Pan. My plan is to never grow up and need senior living." I empathized with both.

Then I spoke with a neighbor and friend who is a role model. "My plan is to place my deposit on a continuing care community in three years, when I'm fifty-five, and to move when I'm around seventy," explained Pier Carlo, now fifty-two. "The communities I'm interested in have long waiting lists, so I want to get my name in there early." He's come to know this through experience, too. "On every Fourth of July, my mother would begin her phone call with 'What do we treasure?' The correct answer was, 'Our independence.' I know what my mother meant, but I think she was sorely misguided. It's a good thing also to celebrate our dependence, and in fact I think it's crucial in order to assure ourselves of comfort in our senescence."

Other friends, especially those in their sixties and seventies, seem paralyzed when it comes to making similar decisions. When I raised the topic of senior living with a neighbor in her late seventies, she just crossed her arms and raised them to her face, signaling that our conversation had ended. Perhaps Pier Carlo should talk to her: "The thing with aging is that you have to be active rather than reactive; you can't wait to move until you have to move because by then you won't be in any condition to tolerate that kind of upheaval." As for aging at home, a recent *New York Times* article stated what few dare to say aloud: Aging at home may be okay for the parents, but it's a nightmare for their kids, who may be thousands of miles away.

Like 90 percent of older Americans, I, too, had hoped to "age in place." That changed when I saw up close how difficult it was for my parents (and how worrisome for my brother, sister, and me). It's also expensive: By the time you're in your sixties, premiums for long-term-care policies average $2,700 a year, according to the industry research firm LifePlans. That ain't cheap, and if you miss a payment, you forfeit every payment made.

Premiums skyrocket as people get older, and once you develop a medical condition, you may be rejected. As for Medicare, forget it. It doesn't cover nursing homes, assisted living, or in-home care.

Fortunately, I live in an area with many housing options, including continuing care communities, nursing homes for those who need more medical care, memory units for people with dementia or Alzheimer's, and co-housing (independent units with shared kitchens and other common areas).

I wondered which, if any, might feel right for a silver-haired guy like me.

To answer that, I kept in mind what an AARP vice president had suggested to me during an interview: It's important to look at future options through the lens of who you'll be in ten or twenty years, not who you are today.

Believe me, I really didn't want to look into that future. But I know that is the nature of denial.

I started my search by booking a tour of a nearby continuing care community that has a waiting list of up to fourteen years, depending on the type of unit. Continuing care communities are among the most expensive options, with entry fees that can reach into several hundred thousand dollars and additional monthly fees from $2,000 to $4,000, reports myLifeSite, which provides a wealth of information about these communities.

Before the tour, I stopped in at the two-bedroom cottage where my friend Debbie Finn, a former teacher, lives with her husband, Arthur, a retired doctor. They miss their old neighborhood and home, where they lived for three decades, but Debbie, now eighty-six, says, "we did the right thing."

"Aging in place is not convenient if one has to go to the hospital and the spouse has to transport them," Debbie—who is fit, stylish, and engaging—told me over lunch. "Reliable help in the home is not easy to come by consistently. Now our children are relieved of all concerns regarding our health needs." I knew, however, that her "kids"—all adults in midlife—had been upfront in expressing their support, no matter what decision their parents made.

Debbie had taken me to eat in the community dining room, which was bright and airy, with lunch choices from shrimp scampi to pizza, to a bountiful salad and sandwich bar. As I looked around the room, I couldn't help but think, "Jeez, there are a lot of old people here!" as I noted the number of residents in wheelchairs, with others relying on canes, walkers, and rollators. I mentioned that to Debbie, who laughed nervously, and then agreed. When I mentioned this experience to another friend, whose mother had been in a different retirement community, she didn't miss a beat in telling me: "Retirement community dining rooms are not a treat. Do not take people there."

This is my future, I thought with a pang.

Undaunted, I persevered and went on to see the rest of the community buildings with a tour group of about twenty. Daughters with their mothers. Couples in their seventies, and a handful older. The ex-husband of a neighbor, in his early eighties, happened to be on the tour and whispered to me before it started, "I'd rather kill myself than be here." He was joking. I think.

Together we visited several units, from a "villa" to regular apartments, all clean and well kept. Some were large and open, others small and claustrophobic, none of them cheap.

My anxiety rose proportionately as my Peter Pan syndrome dissolved: Yes, I would be one of these old people one day. Would that fear inspire me to plan—or to adopt my parents' denial? Before the tour continued on to the skilled nursing facility, a euphemism for those in their final chapter, I had my answer: I ran out the back door without saying goodbye.

I continued my search. Next, I looked into a cohousing community, an option that's less expensive, but still not exactly affordable housing. Cohousing communities, a relatively new option for seniors, feature private apartments or town houses that share common spaces like kitchen, dining, laundry, and entertainment areas. Charles Durrett, an architect who coined the name and who has cowritten *The Senior Cohousing Handbook*, explained that community participation among residents is fundamental to cohousing. One self-described "happy resident" made a point to tell me, "It's an excellent choice for seniors to house themselves with dignity, independence, safety, mutual concern—and fun."

"There's no hierarchy among the residents," Durrett told me, adding that the facilities are designed to foster community and connection. "It's not just about independence and care—it's about the all-important emotional

well-being of each and every one." In many of these communities, the residents do much of the day-to-day
caregiving for each other when needed. Sure, I could food
shop and make dinner for a neighbor. But frankly, I
couldn't imagine changing a resident's adult diaper or—
worse—having someone down the hall do so for me.
That's a bit too much connection for me.

I understand better now why my parents couldn't
make a plan, even though they'd been fortunate enough
to have the ability to pay for almost any level of care. We'd
seen my great-aunt live out her final days in a nursing
home, and I will forever remember the row of residents,
in wheelchairs, lined up in a dark hallway, their heads
drooped, their mouths agape. It's terrifying to contem-
plate one's own old age. I love my current house (with a
ground-floor bedroom and bath, making it feasible for
aging in place). But without a spouse (at least for now), I
knew I needed a Plan B and mailed in a deposit for the
continuing care community. I'm relieved, and I'm guessing that my three nieces will be, too.

I Won't Let a Walker Ruin My Style (but I'll Still Use It)

I'm putting my faith in the design world to come up with better-looking walkers by the time I need one. When that day comes, I hope to rock (and roll) my rollator with style.

"THE WALKER, AS AN ACCESSORY, wrecks every outfit." At least, that's what a high school friend told me after her "stylish" and "vain" mother refused to use one. When her mom claimed the walker was too ugly to use, this friend explained, "We tarted it up with a plum-colored mesh pouch to hold her *New York Times*, lipstick, purse, all attached with bright green rubber ties." It didn't help. Her mom still refused the walker.

Ah, the dreaded walker and all it represents with every turn of its little wheels: loss of independence, vigor, and strength. It screams "doddering" and, as if all that weren't bad enough, it's plug-ugly, to be sure. No wonder so many older people resist the walker; it offends on so very many levels.

When it came to my dapper dad—with his mod sideburns in the 1960s and his black turtlenecks in the 1970s—I had long assumed that he refused a walker because it marked him as an old man. An invalid. I'd never, frankly, considered how much he must have hated the walker's effect on his personal style. Sometimes there's much to be said for the superficial.

Some product developers have tried to improve the no-frills walker, but without much success. A caregiver I know (let's call her "Mary") suggested, without sarcasm, "Make it pretty and lovely so she's proud to be seen with it." In fact, Mary noted that the decorations could be seasonal: colorful silk leaves in autumn, holly and ivy in December, hearts in February, and four-leaf clovers for St. Patrick's Day. I wasn't sold on the notion that decorating a symbol of old age in the style of a kindergarten classroom would save anyone's pride.

Reflecting on my high school friend's challenge in getting her mom to use a walker and thinking back on how Dad had fought it, I decided to do a Google search for "How to decorate a walker." Clearly, I was on to something, since my search delivered an astounding fourteen million results. I couldn't resist clicking on a YouTube video called—demonstrating little imagination—"How to decorate a walker!" A company named Shrinkins, which sells "snazzy" wrapping paper that can be affixed to the walker, produced it. "Applying Shrinkins to your medical device is as easy as 1-2-3—just wrap it, tape it, and shrink it with your blow dryer," reads the advertisement. In case anyone's wondering, these stick-on papers (would you like stylish leopard or zebra?) can also be applied to crutches, canes, IV poles, plaster casts, and even wheelchairs.

I found the whole concept to be ridiculous, like putting lipstick on a pig. As long as walkers look like the bathtub benches and commode lifts they're often sold alongside, they will continue to wreck outfits—and our psyches.

That's why I'm delighted that a slew of new and enthusiastic designers, many from Scandinavia, are updating the traditional walker and rollator (the four-wheeled version with a seat), both functionally and aesthetically. Take the Let's Fly model, which looks like the love child of an elegant midcentury-modern chair and a high-tech folding scooter; it won top prize as "the most beautifully designed product" at one European industry exhibit. Let's Fly also comes with high-style accessories, including a matching tote, so you won't be one of those people with a plastic bag twisting in the wind on the handle of your ugly walker.

So yes, style matters, but in my tussle with Dad I discovered that language does, too. Before the walker imbroglio, my siblings and I suggested that Dad start using a *cane*. He refused, going so far as to show us what he'd come up with when he Googled "canes": "Old people walking sticks and canes, for the disabled, elderly care."

Looking over his shoulder, I saw that many of the entries on Amazon smartly referred to "canes" as "walking sticks." Aha! A walking stick conjures up visions of an English gent, spaniel by his side, strolling around his estate—not an old man hobbling down a nursing home corridor with a cane.

Dad wasted no time in ordering his wooden "walking stick," which he found quite to his liking. Stubborn old guy that he was, though, the stick rested against the wall in his bedroom, regardless of where he was in the house.

I decided to try reason (and maybe a little fear), so one afternoon I sat down with my father, a rational man about almost everything. I told him that using a walking stick would actually help him remain independent, so that he'd be able to get around without help. I even showed him the results of a study titled "Do Canes or Walkers Make Any Difference?" where, in a word, the answer was *yes*. The study found that three-quarters of respondents who had fallen "were not using their device at the time . . . despite stating that canes help prevent falls." Why would people who understood a cane could prevent falls not use one? I read the top four reasons aloud to Dad: I actually don't need it. I forgot I had one. It made me feel old. It's never close by.

Dad quickly changed the subject—a strategy and retort I'd later use myself when asked a difficult question—wanting to know what we were having for dinner.

I reminded Dad that his own mother had also rejected a cane despite a number of falls. Driven by equal parts independence and obstinacy, Grandma, at age eighty-four, continued to ride the New York City subways. It hardly came as a surprise when one afternoon she was knocked flat on her back on the E train (ironically part of the old IND, or Independent, line). Grandma spent her last year in a hospital, having sacrificed all of her independence by refusing the help of a cane. She returned home only to die, two days after being discharged.

Yes, my genetic line carries a big streak of stubborn, and I vow I'll never be like those people. Really, I won't.

I Won't Smell Like
a Decrepit Old Man

It's bad enough when the daily shower becomes more of a daily grind, or when laundry baskets are too heavy to tote. Now science has given us something else to pay attention to: the chemical source of that old-person smell.

"IF I CAN'T TAKE CARE of my personal grooming anymore, I will find help," a friend of mine in her sixties swore to me. "At the very least, I want to be clean—and smell fresh—so people sit by me and hold my hand."

I know. I, too, want to make sure I never develop that unmistakable "old-person smell." Yes, that's a real thing, and it's actually been studied in scientific research laboratories. "Elderly people really do have a distinct scent, so recognizable in fact that people can identify them by body odor alone," said a report in *Time* magazine. I can recall my grandmother's scent more than thirty-five years after her death. Regardless of whether she had showered (and she didn't on a daily basis, not uncommon among her generation), Grandma exuded a mildly sweet and musty odor. Part of her scent was powered by Jergens Original Scent skin lotion, known to generations for its "cherry almond essence." But there was also a decided layer of just *old*.

Each of us tend to have different odors at different ages, starting with the fresh scent of a newborn (which is said be appealing to moms and help with infant bonding). Compare that with the smell of a teenage boy going through puberty (whose stinky hormones may be a mating call to signal fertility or sexual prowess). Consciously or not, we humans get a lot of information from the smell of others.

"Similar to other animals, humans can extract signals from body odors that allow us to identify biological age, avoid sick individuals, pick a suitable partner, and distinguish kin from non-kin," said Johan Lundström, a sensory neuroscientist at the Monell Chemical Senses Center, in a press release about a study he led. Young people were asked to evaluate different body odors (without knowing the age of the person who generated the odor). Unexpectedly, Lundström found they did not mind the smell of older people. While old-person smell is often considered unpleasant, "it is likely that the body odors originating from the old individuals would have been rated as more negative if participants were aware of their true origin." Aha—we are only turned off by old-person smell when we know it comes from an old person.

The same study also reported that participants rated the odors of older people as "less unpleasant" and "less intense" than, say, those stinky teenage boys. Duh.

The study design is actually fascinating, albeit a little gross. Nearly four dozen men and women were divided into three age-groups: young (20 to 30), middle-aged (45 to 55), and old (75 to 90). For five consecutive days, the subjects wore the same undershirt, each of which came specially outfitted with an underarm pad to absorb body odor. At the end of day five, the pads were collected and cut into quarters, with each piece placed in a jar. The study participants were asked to open each jar, smell the pad, and guess the person's age and sex. (Eww, I say, but that's not the point.) Young and middle-aged people smelled too similar to differentiate, but their scents rated high in both "intensity" and "unpleasantness." On the other hand, body odors from the old-age group were rated as "less intense" and "less unpleasant" than their younger counterparts. Now you know.

Actually, there's a scientific explanation for why older people have a distinctive body odor and—surprise!—it has nothing to do with personal hygiene, unwashed sheets and towels, or medications and diet. The culprit is 2-nonenal, a chemical compound with an unpleasant musky and grassy odor. It is only detected in people over forty, with levels increasing with age. Apparently, the lipids found in skin cells start to oxidize more as we age, and the more oxidized lipids on our skin, the greater the level of 2-nonenal we produce.

Bingo!

Distinctive, of course, is not necessarily a bad thing. Is it really just our own bias that leads us to dislike the smell of 2-nonenal? Not too many years ago, *The New York Times* published a first-person essay about a couple in their fifties who had lent their house to an older couple. According to the unhappy author, the older friends left the house "with a distinctive smell in the air." Even though the house appeared spotless, the writer aggressively "wiped countertops and mopped floors" in an attempt to eradicate the smell. No matter how much she cleaned, she wrote, "the odor remained. Not terrible but strange and cloyingly human."

Readers were outraged, asking whether *The Times* would "ever publish an article asking whether Black people smell different, or Hispanics, or fat people, or Gay People. Of course not. Grouping people in any category is just plain bigotry." More evidence as to why ageism is perhaps the last acceptable form of discrimination.

But leave it to the $135 billion skincare industry to come up with a solution to smelly old people—and to reinforce the bias against them in the process. The cosmetic firm Shiseido Group developed a product to neutralize the scent of 2-nonenal ("which is not nice at all," according to the company). Shiseido even takes full credit for coining the term "aging odor," which they claim is "the second most offensive scent behind bad breath." Wow, that's pretty bad.

The product, Harmonage Fragrance, contains persimmon extract, which the maker claims can neutralize "aging odor." Until recently it was widely available in supermarket deodorants as a spray or roll-on, with stick and sheet versions, too. It's most definitely not for women only; Shiseido also made a guy's version. Not to be outdone, another Japanese company, Mirai Clinical, sells a persimmon soap bar that promises not only to end old-person smell but also "troublesome vaginal and foot odors."

Frankly, I think I'll skip the "Febreze for Grandmas" and save my money. I'll keep brushing my teeth, even whitening them. I'll shave until my dying day. I'll regularly use soap and water. And I may even buy some Jergens Original lotion with cherry almond scent—I wouldn't mind smelling like my grandmother, and I'll bet someone would hold my hand if I did.

I Won't Whine About How Much Things Cost

Complaining about the cost of everything seems to be woven into the very fabric of old age. Yes, prices continue to rise faster than pension and Social Security checks do, but I will accept that as inevitable and not become prickly about it. (Except, maybe, about the cost of iPhones.)

NOT TOO LONG AGO, I came across a really mean-spirited blog titled "Why Do Old People Seem to Feel Entitled to Complain About Prices?" The comment section was spirited, to say the least, but one post in particular made me want to register a complaint about its querulous young seller, whose price for a particular product was lower than that of others offering the same product, but who was still allegedly receiving complaints from old people. "It bothers me that the complaint is ignorant, but [it's even worse]...that they are arrogant enough to complain in the first place."

Why such hostility? Is this a knee-jerk reaction to the "When I was your age . . . kids behaved better, food tasted better, and, yes, a buck was really a buck" complaint voiced by so many older people? (And its perfect corollary: "I walked ten miles to school, uphill both ways." Yes, old folks lived in harder, if cheaper, times.)

I beg of my contemporaries: Please stop complaining about the high cost of living these days. I know it's not easy, but stop. In my case, the urge to complain is genetic. I'll start by blaming my grandmother, who lived through the Great Depression and spent her life counting every penny. Grandma kept meticulous ledgers for more than sixty years, many of which I've inherited. Each week, in her distinctive penmanship, she'd enter her take-home salary, and that of my grandfather, a tradesman. She would then subtract the weekly expenses, which included food, electricity, phone, gas, and water, and the occasional notations for the sewer tax ($16), a replacement stove and sink ($267), even reporting the purchase of a new girdle in 1951 ($2.60). (And in 1973, she painstakingly entered the funeral expenses for my grandfather—flowers $60, reverend $100, and buffet $52—adding that it was her "saddest year.") Grandma maintained this household ledger from before my dad's birth in 1929 until a year before her death in 1992. Now these ledgers sit on my bookshelf, reminding me of her eternal thriftiness, a trait she also instilled in my dad.

"Anyone who lived through [the Great Depression] realized the contingencies of life and the vulnerabilities," Andrew Achenbaum, a historian of old age at the University of Houston, told *The New York Times*. Describing people like my father, who had worked his way into the middle class, Achenbaum continued, "there was always this lurking fear that everything could turn around in a second.... It made them edgier than they would have been otherwise, and it has persisted throughout their lives."

Amen, my poor dad. He lived in terror of economic catastrophe, pouring cheap scotch into premium bottles, making his mother's Depression-era kielbasa recipe, and always buying our family's holiday tree on Christmas Eve, when they'd go on sale. I remember how Dad, horrified by "city prices," would drive from Manhattan to some Godforsaken tree lot in Brooklyn for our less-than-perfect (but still-beautiful-in-its-own-way), twice-marked-down tree. (To be fair, Dad always worked hard, paying for my wire braces, summer camps, and most of my college education.)

Alas for me, it appeared that I hadn't inherited any of my ancestors' frugality. It took me until my fortieth birthday to pay off all my college loans and those hefty credit card balances—mostly from "essential businesses" like Bloomingdale's, Lord & Taylor, and Brooks Brothers. "How many sweaters do you need?" was a constant refrain from my mom, who also inquired on a regular basis (even though I used my own MasterCard): "How much did *that* cost?"

But then, at age fifty, that genetic switch flipped on in me. During the Great Recession of 2008, I became hyperaware of the cost of goods: Like my dad, I, too, began looking for bargain-priced Christmas trees.

I'd not only become frugal like my grandmother and father before me, I heard my mother's voice exit my mouth when I asked one of my nieces that most vexing question—"How much did *that* cost?"—referring to the iPhone she'd just bought—even though it was none of my business, nor was I paying for it. Sins of the grandparents, the parents, and now the uncle.

I promise I will bite my tongue when it comes to how expensive things are becoming. But seriously, $1,000 for a new iPhone?

I Won't Play
the Age Card

Yes, age allows some privileges, like movie discounts and (maybe) a seat on the bus, but it's not a free pass. I deserve the respect owed to all elders, but preferential treatment has its limits. Older people—like younger ones—need to curb their sense of entitlement.

I ADMIT THAT I'M STILL NOT entirely comfortable with my senior discounts. Asking for a senior-priced ticket at the movies or a museum, or pulling out my AARP card when checking in to a qualifying hotel, is a bit like trumpeting "I'm old!" to the cashier, and to anyone within hearing distance. Still, a discount is a discount, and I'll take it—even if I use my "inside voice" to request it.

In that vein, I confess: I've become an obsessive follower of Brad's Deals, an online shopping site. As one fan posted, "I don't know who said getting older was a bad thing, but they obviously didn't know anything about these amazing senior discounts!" Thanks to these deals,

I know to ask for my discount when I indulge myself at Ben & Jerry's, Krispy Kreme, or Burger King. Offers aplenty for both men's and women's fashion exist at retailers from coast to coast. I can usually find senior discount coupons for airlines, hotels, and cruise lines. To all these merchants, I say thank you.

Alas, even with all these generous retailers who offer us a break, there are plenty of Boomers who feel entitled to even more. A couple posted angrily on Brad's Deals, "We deserve a discount on everything, everywhere, every time." One woman denounced the Brad's Deals web team for using a blue background when it posted replies to shopper questions to distinguish them from the hundreds of posts from users: "Why would you put this kind of list online and then use blue to highlight since blue doesn't print unless you print in color which is more expensive and this whole thing is about saving money?????" My response: Please stop with this nonsense.

The scales finally tipped for me when a woman complained about having difficulty buying black diamond earrings. "I can't get the deal to come through and I really want three pair." Oh yes, I felt for her . . . in a very "first world problem" kind of way.

Not surprisingly, I found plenty of backlash against these whiners. "Don't expect everyone to do what you want because 'you are older.' Respect is earned not demanded . . . GRRRRRR," commented a not-so-old person on a thread called "entitled old people." Actually, this post was one of *thousands* more just like it, many complaining that seniors feel they deserve deference and service— without being required to say a simple thank-you: Sorry, fellow Boomers, but I'm with the backlash here—let's stop with the entitlement, already.

Facing off with strangers online is one thing, but when the clash between generations happens among family members, it can be even more painful. In one online advice column, a daughter asked for help dealing with her eighty-something widowed mother, who lived "independently" at home. That independence came with a price—but Mom wasn't paying. Her daughter wrote:

> Mom expects everyone else to take on her responsibilities of being able to live independently. Food shopping. House cleaning. Meal prep. It doesn't matter to her that she's still capable of doing a lot of things for herself. It really irks me that she feels entitled to this help because of her age and doesn't want to pay for any services, even though she has the finances to do it. This sense of entitlement has cost her friendships, and now family members are starting to back away. I cannot possibly take this all on. Any advice?

I'll answer for her here:

> Dear Mom—Use your AARP and Medicare cards; after all, you've earned your senior discounts. But please curb your entitlement. It's hard for me to say 'no' to you, but I have other obligations, like my job and my family, and sometimes, I have to. I hope you can understand that I cannot take this all on, but I can help you come up with a plan.
>
> Love, Your Daughter

I Won't Forget
My Manners

This is more a hope than a promise, since I know etiquette can fade as the brain fails. I will do my best to remember my table manners (and please and thank you) as long as I can—and hope for the kindness of friends and family when I can't.

MY MOTHER WAS A STICKLER for proper etiquette, and she taught me to be well mannered from the time I was a child. Perfect table manners were a given, but it didn't end there. When I was still a teen, Mom bought me my first set of personal Crane stationery, engraved with my name, so that I could write proper thank-you notes to relatives and friends for gifts. She bought a matching set for herself, and I remember the afternoons we'd sit side by side and write our thank-yous. We were two polite peas in a very proper pod.

That's what made it so shocking when, soon after she was diagnosed with lung cancer in her early eighties,

Mom's personality began to shift. She stopped saying please and thank you, and my prompts did nothing to ameliorate the situation. I barely recognized her at the table, where she used her hands instead of a fork, a faux pas that she never would have allowed. And then, one afternoon, frustrated and in pain, Mom called her Black health aide "a Georgia slave." All hell broke loose, as the aide reported the verbal assault to the agency. Instead of being repentant, Mom grew indignant that people were making such a big deal about it. I tried to reason with Mom. "It was only a joke," she replied. "It's not funny, Mom. You hurt Sheila." I could not understand how this well-mannered woman, a lifelong liberal, didn't realize that her comment was racist.

Not that Mom was ever much for apologizing. My mother could swear like a sailor when she felt provoked (which she frequently did), and it was no fun to be on the receiving end. It mattered not at all whether she was right or wrong, like the time she denounced the neighbor whose *parked* car she'd hit, accusing him of being wrong rather than apologizing for having backed into his car. But her hellcat habits never had never interfered with her manners—and she experienced not one whit of cognitive dissonance about that until her cancer diagnosis.

Eventually, it became clear that Mom was developing dementia, as she grew more disoriented and combative. She'd insist that we were at the beach house when, in fact, she was in her apartment in the city. Initially, I challenged her, often starting with a plaintive "Mom!" and ending with a "damn it." This wasn't the mother I knew.

And frankly, I wasn't the person I usually am. Together, we were one stressed-out, horribly unmannered pair.

Mom's inner spitfire would come alive when I challenged her, and her tongue became wicked as never before. One day, she insisted on going to the emergency room and had her health aide call 911 (Sheila, stalwart that she was, had stayed on). But once at the ER, Mom wanted only to flee. She called me from the hospital—I was at home hundreds of miles away—and after speaking with the nurse on duty, I explained to Mom that she needed to complete the tests they'd started. Then she let me have it: "You're a terrible son. How could you do this to me, especially after everything I've done for you?"

I was heartbroken. Confused. Hurt. Angry. I tried to be compassionate, but as time went by, Mom got nasty and kept pushing my buttons. I was not always my kindest self to her, and that haunted me. It still does. Her dementia may have explained her lost manners, but what did I have to explain mine? I know that, more than anything, I was trying to hold on to the mother I'd known my whole life. It was so hard to watch her slowly leave us.

I began to fear my mother's outbursts; they embarrassed me and hurt others. I began to understand that this disease had changed her; it was the illness that made her mean and ill-mannered. And yet, even with that knowledge, I often found it difficult to be patient and understanding. I began to notice that she couldn't manage multiple tasks, follow through on anything, or consider the consequences of her actions. The filter or internal "governor" that once prevented her—as it does most of us—from saying and doing inappropriate things had begun to break down.

Toward the end of her life, my mother softened, and she became the best version of herself—more considerate and kind. She even became more forgiving. (My siblings and I often joked, "Who *is* this woman?") We never really understood this shift, but it made day-to-day life much easier. The only clue I could decipher was a question she asked with increasing frequency: "How will I be remembered?" This led her to understand how admitting fault opened the door to atonement and forgiveness—and didn't make her powerless at all. When she finally apologized to Sheila for her outburst, it was muddled. Still, I could sense Mom's relief in thinking she had resolved the situation, as well as a self-satisfaction in having stepped up. (She never did apologize to the neighbor whose car she wrecked.)

In my research on dementia, I've seen a torrent of angry posts on eldercare sites and caregiver forums complaining about the terrible—really horrific—manners of aging parents. Yes, they chew with their mouths open, wipe their hands on the tablecloth instead of a napkin, and pick up food meant to be eaten with utensils. Having been raised on perfect table manners, I understand the horror. But having witnessed my mom's dementia up close, I also understand the need for what I call "one-way etiquette" and kindness. I've learned not to be upset when someone with memory issues makes a faux pas— or worse. They've earned their Get Out of Jail Free card for any manners misdemeanors or felonies.

It all made me realize anew how important our little civilities are in life—but also that civility cuts both ways. Yes, I hope to continue to be well mannered, kind, and respectful until the end of my days, but my mind may not allow that. That's when I hope my loved ones don't turn the tables on me—I'm counting on them to use some "one-way etiquette" to preserve my dignity.

I Won't Be Ordering the Early Bird Special

Nothing says "old" like "three course menu nightly, 4:30 P.M. to 6 P.M., $18.99." My promise to stick with dining after dark is also a nod to the parable of the boiling frog: I will remember to jump out of the hot pot before I cook myself into 9 P.M. bedtimes, sedentary habits, and a self-imposed lockdown (that has nothing to do with COVID-19).

REMEMBER THE *SEINFELD* EPISODE where Jerry berates his parents for eating dinner in the afternoon? In case it's lost in a back room of your mind, here's a quick refresher: Morty and Helen, now retired to Florida, have discovered the ubiquitous "early bird special," but Jerry's having none of it.

> JERRY: "Four-thirty? Who eats dinner at four-thirty?" . . .
>
> HELEN: "We gotta catch the early bird. It's only between four-thirty and six."

MORTY: "Yeah. They give you a tenderloin, a salad, and a baked potato for $4.95. You know what that costs you after six?"

When I was growing up, other moms in our predominantly Jewish neighborhood cooked from scratch, sitting down to their brisket and kasha suppers at 5 P.M. Not so in our family. Our Mom's *nom de cuisine* became "shake 'n bake" because she—and we—loved the wildly popular bread crumb–style coating for chicken—not to mention the jingle: "Why fry? Shake 'n Bake!" We'd laugh all over ourselves, as did our friends, who coveted dinner invitations from the Petrows. But everything came with a price: Dinner hour at our house was practically Continental: 7 P.M.

For decades, the family dinner hour remained the same, although Mom's culinary repertoire expanded to include new favorites, a decidedly eclectic mix, like chicken cacciatore, oxtail stew, and ham steaks with grilled pineapple. But once my parents crossed the threshold to seventy, the dinner bell began to ring earlier and earlier. At first, I could hardly tell—after all, what's the difference between 7 P.M. and 6:30? And then it slipped again, becoming 6 P.M. With visits on my part less frequent, I came home one vacation to see Mom starting to prepare "dinner" (scrambled eggs, in this case) at about 4:30 P.M.

"Mom!" I cried out, echoing Jerry Seinfeld's outrage. "Are you crazy? Why are you planning to eat so early?" As was often the case, I heard the *J'accuse* in my voice, but I was also far from hungry (having eaten lunch just three hours earlier). My mother replied, "That's when your father wants to eat."

True that. But I came to notice other changes to their daily routines. My parents slept less and less well. Both started their days earlier, my father often at 6 A.M. Not surprisingly, then, the lunch hour also came earlier, with my mother's decreasing appetite reflecting her declining physical exertion. (Activity creates appetite, and she had very little of either.) Dad became frightened of having to go to the bathroom at night, so he preferred to finish eating—and drinking—with the sun still in the sky.

During their lives I never put together the full picture when it came to my parents' dining habits. Since they died, I've taken solace from many of the online posts I've read. "Dinner at 4 p.m. was just the tip of the iceberg that was about to sink his ship," wrote a blogger in a post aptly titled "Do you ever wonder why Dad eats dinner at 4 pm?" With some sleuthing, he realized his father, a widower, had lost interest in most daily activities, got very little exercise, was lonely and isolated, suffered from constipation, had medication interactions that affected his appetite, and didn't want to drive or go out after dark. Hello, Mom and Dad.

As I paid closer attention, I began to better understand that changed eating patterns are often a warning sign.

A daughter wrote online, with much of the resentment I'd observed in myself, "I can't stand it. My 82-year-old mother eats dinner at either 3:00 or 4:00 pm. She's driving me nuts because it's impossible to take her out to dinner. If I make the earliest reservation at 5 pm, she's going to be ready by 3:30, impatient to leave. I explain over and over that they're not serving yet. Then, when it's time to leave, she refuses to go. Fine. I'll go without her and enjoy a meal on my own, which is far more pleasant than eating with her and listening to her complaints about everything. Which is nothing new."

I wonder if the daughter understood that leaving her mother to eat alone increased the likelihood of depression, a leading cause of poor nutrition among the elderly. Or that the sight, smell, and taste of food that used to make eating enjoyable often diminish with age.

Finally, before I finished reading the online posts, this comment from a Millennial stopped me cold:

"My grandparents adhere to a very strict routine. They eat their meals on a schedule. Any variation from this schedule upsets them and makes them very grouchy. Why do they have to be so rigid? Why can't they have their meals at normal times and have snacks in between meals if they are hungry? My complaint isn't the time, but that they have no flexibility. I hope I'm not like that when I get old."

I hope I'm not like that, too. But this young man's reprimand reminded me of the parable of the boiling frog, which one of my yoga instructors tells from time to time as part of her efforts to keep us "awake," or from sleepwalking through life. It goes like this: If you wanted to boil a frog, how would you do it? Sure, you could place the frog in a pot of hot water, but if it's too hot, the frog will jump out to save its life. No, what you need to do is fill the pot with cool water, add the frog, and then slowly heat the water. As the temperature warms, the frog will relax. It's like taking a warm bath. Keep increasing the heat, and the frog will become drowsy as it relaxes more and more. By the time the water is about to boil, it's too late for the frog to take action. It can't escape, and it perishes in the boiling water.

Many interpretations of this parable exist. When it comes to growing older, I understand it as a metaphor cautioning us to be aware of the dangers of slow change, and our unwillingness to react to grave threats unless they are sudden.

Yes, I hope to remain flexible when it comes to the dinner hour, but more than that, I hope that this old frog will be able to tell when the temperature starts to rise and jump before I find myself in hot water—or start eating dinner at 4:30 P.M. Maybe, even, a loved one will help me escape this fate before it's too late.

I Won't Turn My House into a Sweat Lodge

What is it about old people that makes them crank the thermostat up to 85 degrees? Rather than bring visitors into a sweat lodge, I'll pile on the layers to keep myself warm without bringing everyone else to the boiling point.

NOT LONG AGO, I ACCEPTED an invitation from a married couple, both in their early eighties, to a dinner at which I knew guests would be—quite literally—in meltdown mode. Even though we were deep in a winter freeze, I wore a short-sleeved cotton shirt under my wool sweater, which I shed immediately upon walking in the door. By the way the other guests had dressed, I could see they'd been to dinner here before as well. One neighbor arrived bundled up in a long down coat, which she removed to unveil a summer sundress—completely inappropriate for the season, but so much more comfortable for dinner with these particular friends. Even lightly clad, at one point she took me aside to say, "I can't breathe here." When I took a bathroom break, I peeked at the thermostat. Yep, 85 degrees—with the forced-air furnace blasting dry heat down our throats and up our nostrils.

"We're so cold," our hosts maintained, as the rest of us shvitzed.

I knew this phenomenon all too well. For the last decade of their lives, my parents could be found shivering during the dog days of August, and that was with the air-conditioning off. It was even worse during the frigid winters, despite the heat being set to "high." I tried subterfuge, slowly turning down the thermostat. I gifted them new accessories, including the coziest of fleece-lined slippers and state-of-the-art Synchilla fleece tops. And I deployed self-pity, making the most of the bloody nose I awoke to one morning after a night spent under a heating vent that baked me dry.

None of it worked—to heighten their awareness or warm their bones.

Two things surprised me. First, my parents—like those dinner hosts—had no clue that their internal thermostats had gone haywire. And second: This common complaint is not another case of old people being obstinate. Truth be told, there are medical reasons why we feel colder as we age. Heart disease, diabetes, and thyroid problems can all impact our internal body temperature. So can various medications, which can lead to reduced blood flow and increased heat loss. Even without those medical conditions, it's a fact: Over time, many of us lose our ability to regulate our body temperatures. As we age, we may also become more sensitive to cold, especially in our hands and feet. These two simple truths can easily turn any older person's home into an Easy-Bake Oven.

I poked around online and came across many similar stories. "For the past three years, my 100-year-old mother says she's freezing even when the heat is up to 90 degrees. I'll give her a sheet and blanket, and then she sweats so much that the chair or sofa she's on is completely wet," posted a "cold-hearted" daughter.

Among my own friends, one told me this unsettling story: "My aunt used to keep her house so warm that once at a party there, I could not figure out what one of her appetizers was. It looked like meat loaf surrounded by crackers. It turns out it was steak tartare that had 'cooked' in the heat of her house!"

Then it had begun with my parents. I'd walk into the sweat lodge they called home and shout to my dad, "Don't you remember we went through this with Grandma?" "No," was his frequent and final answer. And then I had to ask myself: When I'm older and bone cold, will *I* remember these conversations with my dad?

For now, I do. But instead of roasting my friends alive when my personal thermostat goes haywire, I'll be turning to thermal underwear, layers of tops, even a ski hat, and a constant infusion of hot tea (but not alcohol) to keep me toasty. I'll even put on an extra pair of socks. And I'll turn down the thermostat ten degrees and try to remember to ask my guests, "Is it too warm for you?"

I Won't Repeat
Stories More Than
One Hundred Times

There's power in personal or family lore—the stories we tell and retell over years and decades. I will generously share my stories with those willing to hear them, and—even more important—I will know when to stop. I hope.

"STOP ME IF I'VE TOLD you this before . . ."

Why do people who start a story with this prelude never actually stop when everyone in the room nods yes, that they've heard it once, twice, thrice, or more?

I've never needed to say it myself (wink, wink), especially not before I launch into one of my best tales, because I'm a big believer in sharing the stories of our lives. It's a way that we convey who we are and what matters to us. Many of my friends know better than to try to stop me once I'm on a roll, but I've witnessed others who've worked out ways (from the polite to the not-so nice) to cut off a repeater. One good friend of mine doesn't use words, but she has a signal shared with her inner circle: "When one of us begins telling a story for the second time, the listeners raise two fingers. If it's the third time, three fingers. If it's the fourth or more, we make the sign of an X!"

My friend Eva says that when her grandmother would start telling a story for the 100th time, she'd call out, "Beep!" to make her stop. Even so, she told me, "I tried to listen when I could. And sometimes I'd learn something new by how she told it. In fact, learning about her past helped unlock a few mysteries about myself."

That's the thing, we need to tell our stories. Again and again. It's actually a perfectly natural phenomenon, with a purpose. Stories that we repeat often are the ones that reflect important values, lessons, or sentiments. They're also a way that we secure our legacy to future generations.

For instance, my dad enjoyed telling his kids (or anyone, actually) the tale of his adventure on a U.S. Coast Guard cutter across the top of Russia (replete with icebergs, polar bears, and a menacing Soviet warship). I recall his first telling it to my third-grade class, along with a vivid slideshow. There was "the constant harassment" from the Soviet forces, "the diplomatic furor the trip aroused," and "the text of a series of unpublished diplomatic exchanges that passed between the two governments, revealing the nature of a long-standing and bitter dispute."

How can I quote Dad word for word from a story told to my class five decades ago? Well, he also wrote it up in his first book (*Across the Top of Russia*), for one thing.

And I probably heard him tell it no fewer than fifty times in his lifetime.

In many ways, this story defined my father. It was a milestone in his professional life; it was a reflection of his character as an explorer and "iron man"; and later in life, it served as a poignant memory of who he had been. Sure, the details varied over the years. For example, "Each sighting of a bear," Dad had written, "was piped on [the] ship's public address system to alert crew." In his later retellings, those polar bears encroached closer and closer to the crew's makeshift ice village, finally trespassing to the point where Dad and his crewmates might become "dinner."

I never challenged Dad (by rolling my eyes or groaning, "I've heard this a hundred times before!") when he'd begin this story. As time went by, the past became even more important to my father, and he began to tell it more frequently. He knew he was repeating it. I knew it. We all did. There was nothing wrong with his memory.

I learned to listen. To be patient. Each time he told it, by his tone and what he stressed, I understood a bit more about him.

I, too, have my own story. I won't tell much of it here, except to say it involved my best friend; a wall of water; a bridge wiped out; and a caravan of cars washed out to sea. An online news story reported it simply as "The Heavy Rain Event of 29 October 2000 in Hana, Maui." Now, two decades past, it's a reflection of how I understand my own character and an indelible memory of a longtime friendship saved by a heroic rescue. Each time I tell it, like my dad, I'm saying, "You don't know all of me. This is part of who I am."

One last tale before I forget.

A dear friend told me about the visits to her grandmother, when dementia had robbed the older woman of her fabled Irish storytelling. "An hour-long visit with her," my friend said, "was really more like one five-minute visit, twelve times in a row. But I would listen and react every time as if it were the first time I'd heard her. She had given me a lifetime of wonderful family stories to remember, and I was grateful for every chance to spend time with her and hear her tell them, even if they were reduced to snippets by then."

I can only hope that if my stories are ever so reduced, I'll have someone to sit and listen—and that my stories will still hold some power and insight into who I am. And who I was.

I don't want to be the old man who makes the room groan when he launches into the same old story yet again, but I do very much want to be the passer-on of family legends, the stories that will keep us alive in the minds and memories of the next generation. I also like to think that by staying active and engaged, I will always have a new supply of stories to tell, from last week and last month, and not have to rely on the ones from the last century for small talk.

I Won't Be Unkind to Those with Dementia

First my mom, then my dog, taught me how to be more compassionate to those whose minds slip away long before their bodies give out. And I won't hesitate to use humor to make my way through it.

I COULD HEAR THE MOURNFUL WAILING from the street as I approached my house. No question about it, that was my Zoe "singing the blues." Once inside, I found my sixteen-year-old Jack Russell terrier in the kitchen, staring blankly at the wall as she continued her plaintive tune.

She'd had various odd behaviors for a year now: getting lost in the house, stuck in corners, urinating on rugs—and that sorrowful howling. It was heartbreaking. The vet kept telling me there was no definitive test, no way to make an official diagnosis. But she agreed with what I knew in my heart: Zoe had dementia.

"Hey Zoe, I'm here!" I shouted to her that day as I entered the house. No reaction (she was largely deaf by that time). In a now-familiar routine, I got down on my knees so that she could see me, and I reached out to softly rub her ear. She loved that, and leaned into my hand as her way of saying "thank you."

Many of Zoe's symptoms and behaviors were all too familiar to me. I had seen them before, in my mother, as she declined into dementia in her final years.

The first time I feared something was amiss with my mother came years before she was diagnosed with dementia. One bright summer day, Mom answered the kitchen phone, and I could hear my friend Holly asking, "May I speak to Steven?" I was standing right next to Mom, her much-loved firstborn home for a visit. Before the phone rang, we'd been gabbing about what to make for dinner that night. I'd volunteered to fire up the barbeque, grilling chicken, corn, and some sweet summer tomatoes.

"There's no Steven here," Mom replied sharply to Holly.

Abruptly, I grabbed the phone from her and chirped, "Hello!"

Holly's question: "Is your mother okay?"

I really didn't know, but I lied to cover for her. "Oh yes, there's a lot of activity here with the grandkids," I said. "I don't think she heard you."

Actually, none of the grandchildren were visiting that afternoon.

After hanging up with Holly, I questioned Mom with some exasperation. "What's the matter with you?" I demanded. "I was right here!" She looked at me blankly, as if she didn't understand, and she didn't answer. Now I realize she must have felt ashamed in addition to her confusion—her mind was starting to slip. It must have been terrifying for her and embarrassing to reveal herself to me that way. To make matters worse, I didn't understand this vexing, saddening first.

The following year Mom forgot my birthday—an event that, at least in her mind, had always been a Major National Holiday.

She was disappearing in plain sight.

By the time my terrier developed dementia, Mom had passed. For the first nine months after I noticed those telltale symptoms in the dog, I'd been able to keep her condition on the down low. Like Mom, Zoe had both good days and bad ones, and I felt as if I were conspiring with her to keep up appearances. Then, one early fall day, my four-legged girl meandered on her own out of the front yard and down the street, a walk we took together every day. Confusion must have set in when she reached the stop sign. She sat down on the pavement, alone and forlorn, and began to howl. My next-door neighbor heard her and quickly alerted me. I ran down the street to scoop her up and bring her home.

Once Zoe was back in my arms, the neighbor asked directly, "How long has she been demented?" The word rang harshly in my ears. Her secret—our secret—was out.

After that incident, I became more vigilant with Zoe: no more letting her out in the yard, no off-leash walks in the park. To calm her, the vet prescribed Prozac, the same medication my mother had taken to quiet her anxiety as she lost her footing in the world.

Still, I found moments of lightness with Zoe, as I had with Mom. On Mom's last birthday, her three kids and one granddaughter took her out for Chinese food, gorging ourselves on egg rolls and egg drop soup, shrimp dumplings, spare ribs, sweet-and-sour pork, roast pork chow mein, and lo mein, too, all doused with excessive amounts of duck sauce. It was hard not to conjure up the past, since takeout Chinese had been one of the major food groups in our family. We laughed with her about our "shake 'n bake" childhood during this lunch, which turned out to be our last one together.

With Zoe, until the very end, we would return home after her morning constitutional, and she would play her favorite game, "kill the squirrel" (which consisted of shaking her squeaky toy rodent by the neck, throwing it high into the air, and then lunging at it when it crashed to earth). Now that she's gone, the squirrels are out in force, dancing on the front porch as if to taunt her for posterity.

In Mom's last voicemail message to me, a week before she died, she lambasted me again, accusing me of having left her the wrong phone number on her answering machine. Of course I hadn't left *any* number, but I felt a familiar anger rise. By then, I understood my real upset was about losing her—not just her mind and spirit, but soon enough all of her, to eternity. Even now, several years after her death, and in my sixties, I joke to my siblings, "I want Mom!" They crack up, but I know our laughter masks our shared pain. They understand.

My mother's illness changed me, teaching me to be more patient and compassionate. I used that as I helped see Zoe through to the end. I sympathized with her confusion, and I did my best to comfort her and reorient her when she became confused. I understood her inconti-nence was not willful, and I placed pee pads strategically around the house. I kept a 64-ounce bottle of "profes-sional strength urine destroyer" to clean up when she messed up. But I also never slept through the night, which left me tired and cranky. Sometimes my emotions spilled over, but never at Zoe. Lessons learned.

I Won't Let Anyone
Treat Me with Disrespect

When it comes to getting older, I don't think anything hurt my dad more than losing the professional status he'd had during his younger years. Thanks to his lessons, I won't let that happen to me, but I will let people know who I am and expect to be treated accordingly.

I'M CERTAIN MY FATHER'S TWO FAVORITE WORDS in the English language were "Professor Petrow." He not only liked the title, he deserved it—he was, after all, a New York University professor for more than three decades. He was also an award-winning author, Emmy Award—winning documentarian, and self-identified "newsman," but above all, he defined himself as a teacher. Over his long tenure at NYU, I remember how he lit up every time one of his students called him Professor Petrow.

Dad retired from NYU in his seventies because of an undiagnosable—and untreatable—neurological ailment that initially affected his "articulation," as he always put it. In the decade before he quit teaching, he visited at least half a dozen top neurologists, including Oliver (*The Man Who Mistook His Wife for a Hat*) Sacks, who assured him in a letter Dad kept and passed on, "You're going to die of another condition many years hence."

Dad's condition didn't turn out to be fatal, but one side effect may have been nearly worse. You see, after his retirement at seventy-five, no one called Dad "professor" anymore; this erasure of his professional identity coincided with the beginning of his slide into infirmity.

By the time he turned eighty, this no-name ailment had progressively weakened the muscles in his arms and legs. His lower body would buckle without warning, and he'd keel over like a giant oak tree crashing down in a storm. His arms, almost useless because of the atrophy of his upper-body muscles, provided no safety net. My mom, my siblings, and I knew the conventional wisdom: falls lead to breaks, and breaks lead to fatalities. We also knew it from experience, because that's just how my grandfather, Dad's father, died in 1976. Disoriented (possibly by his medication), my grandfather tried to climb out of a hospital bed one night. Somehow, he surmounted the rail, only to come tumbling down and break his hip when he hit the floor. We buried him two weeks later.

The whole family was concerned about Dad's increasing frailty, but we weren't sure what to do about it.

One morning, our father sent us all an email with the subject line in all caps: "MAYDAY." The body of it read: "Hello all . . . Need help on a continuing basis."

Dad had never asked for help before, so we stepped up. I got access to his online financial accounts and started paying the bills; my brother managed household repairs. Our "baby" sister, a lawyer, became "Executive Vice President in Charge of F*cking Everything Else."

We did more, and visited more often, but we could never stop his falls. We hired home health aides, but he continued to fall. Even when I was there, I'd hear him fall in another part of the house, despite our pleas that he call for assistance before getting up from a chair or out of bed. Dad was lucky so many times—for years, he never broke a bone, although he suffered contusions and concussions. When I would see a bruise and ask, as gently as I knew how, "What happened, Dad?" he'd reply angrily, "Nothing."

I didn't understand his anger at the time; now I have a better grasp. Nothing was within his control: not his finances, the upkeep of his home, or his wife's health. And his kids kept haranguing him with, "What happened, Dad?"

Eventually, his doctor recommended a walker—advice he ignored—and soon Dad was falling three or four times a day. One night, in the dead of his penultimate winter, Dad had a bad fall on the way to the bathroom. He was naked. His anger exploded, fueled by embarrassment and his increasing disability. Mom could not calm him down. The aide could not get near him because he was flailing like a rabid animal. Mom called me, five hundred miles away, and I called 911. Within ten minutes I heard the sirens through the phone, and I continued to listen as the medics rushed in. The EMTs, bless their hearts, got him up, his bathrobe on, and back into bed. No bones broken. Another crisis averted—or at least put off for another day.

We worried more and more. My brother feared that Dad would fall in the shower, and finally he convinced him to have a grab rail put in. The very next day, Dad called the handyman back. "Take it out!" Our next step: We had a small bench placed in the shower. Dad's response: a growing antipathy to showering.

More than anything, I knew the importance of Dad's independence—just as I knew from years of observing his relationship with our mother that he didn't take direction well. I tried reasoning with him. I tried cajoling him. He "yessed" me time and again, but that was part of his new strategy: lying. He lied about whether he'd fallen. He lied about his pain. Our mother, so ill herself, knew the truth, but was reluctant to call him out on it.

I emailed his psychotherapist for advice. He replied by explaining how deeply challenging it was for an independent and outgoing person like my father to be diminished, to become dependent on others and find his world curtailed. As for advice? He suggested I recognize and allow what my dad could continue to do safely, but when necessary to curb his enthusiasm with respect and sensitivity. And to ask him questions that allowed him to be the decision maker, for instance: "Dad, what do you think is the safest way to . . . ?" The psychotherapist admitted this would be a tough balancing act.

A second health aide joined us in what turned out to be his last full spring, because both of our parents now required heavy lifting. Each morning, I noticed that Hilde would greet Dad by asking, "Professor Petrow, how are you today?" She'd have to have been blind not to see the delight in his face, as would the rest of us. Soon, nearly every sentence from Hilde contained his former honor-ific. "Professor, what would you like for breakfast?" "What time do you want to go for a walk, Professor?" She could even tell him what to do: "Professor, you need to take your medication." And he would.

It had been a long time since I'd seen Dad so pleased, so recognized. I saw the lesson: Treat him as an adult. Respect him and understand his identity.

After he died we made sure that his tombstone honored him properly; it reads:

RICHARD PETROW

1929–2017

PROFESSOR AND JOURNALIST

We chose "professor and journalist" because we understood those words to be a kind of shorthand for who he was—and by that I don't mean just his jobs but his actual sense of identity. And that's the lesson I take from this: I will not let others erase my identity. I will ask to be treated with respect—but will do so as nicely as I can.

I Won't Lose My Balance

Those of us over fifty talk about balance in two ways. There's literal balance, as in: "I will not lose my balance and fall." There's also balance as a metaphor: "I will live my life in balance." I won't give up on either.

M Y EMBRACE OF THE BALANCED LIFE started in the late 1980s, when I read Robert Fulghum's bestselling book *All I Really Need to Know I Learned in Kindergarten*. He exhorted: "Live a balanced life—learn some and think some and draw and paint and sing and dance and play and work every day some."

"Love that," I said to my thirtysomething self. And I did, for years.

A decade older, I came across another version of essentially the same message: "Living in balance is easy and very rewarding because your life becomes one of joy, happiness, and serenity." Now immersed in early-stage midlife skepticism, I muttered, "I'm not so sure how easy that really is."

My turnabout seemed complete by my late fifties, when I found myself in a yoga class, staring down at a green foam block imprinted with: *Life. Balance. Growth.*

"That's bull," I growled with an expletive, loudly enough for the person next to me to throw some shade in my direction. As punishment, I promptly lost my balance, falling out of my pose.

After class, I talked with the yoga instructor about my disenchantment with the entire "balance" incantation. To my surprise, she confessed, "Personally, I think balance is a fallacy. It's presented in society as something that can be achieved, but in reality, it's not an achievable goal."

Really? I decided I needed to take this to a higher power. That was Susan Piver, a Buddhist teacher and the author of *The Wisdom of a Broken Heart*, who has long been a life guide to me. "Is it ever possible to be balanced?" she asked rhetorically when I approached her. "I don't think it is, because then you'd have to freeze in that position. 'Got it. Now don't move.'" Even the noted biologist John Kricher was among the apostates, writing that there "is no balance of nature—not today and not at any time in Earth's long history. The paradigm is based on belief, not data; it has no scientific merit."

My mentors had confounded me. Yet no matter my muddle, I continued my search for balance: a deeper yoga practice, more vacations, a "balanced" diet. I even signed up for a "digital detox" retreat. Its mantra was "Disconnect to Reconnect." The promise: "More mindful, meaningful, and *balanced* [emphasis added] lives." Still, balance remained an unobtainable state, an illusory goal. In fact, the more I desired it, the further it retreated from me.

By age sixty, I had transitioned from believer to heretic. Not only did this aphorism seem inauthentic and unobtainable; even worse, a "balanced" life now sounded monotonous and dull. One Zen-y writer asked: Who would not want a life where you enjoy every second and where you can be happy without any reason to be happy?

I'm raising my hand. I don't.

Looking back on my life, I think I could have read the clues to my future heresy better. After all, I had had a couple of early lessons.

Lesson Number 1: Just before Y2K, I was on the hunt for a pair of bedside table lamps at a local antique shop. Russell, the proprietor, showed me a half-dozen sets, but they were all too large, too gaudy, or too expensive. The pair I actually liked had one obvious flaw: They were different. One was taller than the other (although their shades shared the same butterfly-on-parchment motif). "How would that look to people?" I asked Russell, worrying that they would think I hadn't noticed their different heights or, worse, that I had lost my gay design mojo.

He smiled and asked, "How many people are you expecting to view your bedside lamps?" Pushing me, he added, "Why does it matter if they aren't balanced? They're beautiful in their individuality, and as a pair, perfect in their difference." Unconvinced, I skipped out.

A week later, I returned to the shop and bought the fraternal twins. In bed that first night, I didn't obsess on what made them different; in fact, my changed vantage point obscured their difference altogether. Instead, I delighted in watching the butterflies dance against the orange glow of the light before I clicked both lamps off. In other words, my mismatched lamps taught me that balance is not about symmetry but about perspective, how we see.

Lesson Number 2: More recently, I was in a San Francisco high-rise when a strong earthquake started to rock and roll the office tower. From thirty floors up, I saw the cityscape appear to sway—first left, then right, then back again. But no, the streets of San Francisco were not on the move. What was swaying was the building, purposely designed with what's called "roller bearing" to mitigate lateral seismic shifts. The design allowed the tower to yield to and absorb the quake force without collapsing. As a Caltech scientist explained to me: "It's gotta give." But not too much.

I survived (obviously), climbing back out from under a desk once the temblor stopped. I'll skip more of the engineering gobbledygook, but that earthquake revealed to me that balance is not about stability or rigidity, but the ability to yield and move.

Which brings me to a more recent yoga class: Shortly after my "bull" epiphany, I was in the midst of tree pose, a balancing act that leaves you standing on one leg (your "trunk") with both arms stretched above your head (the "branches"). With my mind wandering, and losing my focus, I started to topple out of the pose. The bamboo floor below me hadn't started to rock or roll, but I had. My first inclination was to lock in my position, which meant to stiffen my joints and tighten my muscles to prevent falling. Or, as Susan Piver had described, I froze.

Just at that moment, I recalled what I had observed during the earthquake. Instead of freezing, I relaxed my muscles and allowed my body to absorb the disequilibrium, which—surprise—allowed me to remain standing tall. Susan later elaborated on what had taken place inside of me: "Balance is not so much striking or holding the pose, but flowing with the movements that affect your pose. The more quickly you can respond and make those adjustments—that's balance. Balance comes from adapting quickly."

Bingo!

Where does this leave me now? My sixties are no time to mindlessly swallow the bromides of our day, which I have learned can be as unbalanced a diet as any. Whether it's falling in yoga class or falling short in life, I can see more clearly now that the coveted state of balance is not about stasis or symmetry but flexibility and change. Anything that challenges my equilibrium, or anyone who tries to throw me off-kilter, will actually improve my balance—because day by day I'm learning to be nimble, deft, and focused.

After all, my balance isn't only a metaphor—I have to be careful not to *literally* fall.

PART III

Stupid Things I Won't Do at "The End"

What makes old age so sad is not that our joys but our hopes cease.

—JEAN PAUL

I Won't Depart This Life Without Someone Holding My Hand

The fear of being old and alone isn't really about who goes with you to medical appointments, it's about isolation and loneliness. I promise I will reach out to others who need a hand or a meal or a ride to the doctor, hoping that I'm paying it forward.

THE COVID-19 PANDEMIC has brought to the fore two of my greatest fears: being sick and being alone. Recently, a neighbor, nearing sixty and single like me, was found dead in his house after not being heard from in several days. Although he had many dear friends, he was by himself when a stroke took his life. Later on, in the many eulogies given for him, friends noted how they'd never been to his house, and just how private he'd been all these years. I jotted down in my journal: I hope not to leave this life without someone holding my hand.

Staring down sixty a few years ago, all my fears about aging came down to this: "Who will take me when I need my colonoscopy?" What I really meant was, I hope I have a lifeline.

It was more than a logistical question. A decade earlier, my husband had ferried me to my first colonoscopy in "celebration" of my turning fifty. As required by the clinic, he remained in the waiting room for several hours, by which time I'd come out of my post–midazolam/propofol/diazepam loopiness. I'd done the same for him two years earlier. But things were different now as I was scheduling my decennial test, as we were in the midst of a divorce.

Our separation could hardly have come at a worse time. My mom had died in January, followed by Dad in April. Jim left me at the midpoint between their deaths. My parents had always been my true north, and in many ways I felt like the "orphan" some of my friends now described me as. Newly single again, in a new home, with my parents gone, I felt unmoored. Adrift. And very much alone.

One of the painful flip sides of Boomers' living longer is that more and more of us are doing so without a spouse or partner. The number of unattached older Americans is nearly twenty million, according to the U.S. Census Bureau. We're likely to live longer than any other generation in history, but 37 percent of older women and 19 percent of older men live alone. The older we get, the worse the odds: A federal survey found that nearly half of women over seventy-five live by themselves.

Or, as the British historian A. J. P. Taylor once wrote: "The greatest problem about old age is the fear that it may go on too long."

As a gay man, I face even worse odds. LGBTQ folks are twice as likely to be single and live alone in our elder years as our straight counterparts, and we are four times less likely to have children. Our families have shunned many of us, while others lost their closest friends to AIDS. Some have never married (in part because it was illegal for so long), while others are widowed or divorced.

Regardless of gender or sexual identity, the worries about future loneliness are universal. As I often do, I turned to Facebook to ask what worried my unpartnered or never-coupled friends as they aged. I was overwhelmed by both the volume of responses and by the commonality of our fears. A divorced friend confessed to worrying "about having to leave my home for assisted living," but many of the fears were of a more everyday variety. One friend in her sixties posted that she had concerns about "shopping, cooking, housekeeping, transportation to medical appointments, handling finances, having sufficient funds." A widowed West Coast teacher of mine added, "it is the smaller, daily things, like a cup of tea and a conversation, that make the difference between feeling well cared for and alone." Many others wrote something similar to another woman's comment, "I am terrified of having to depend on others."

And finally, the mother of all fears: "Being alone, then dying alone."

But wait . . . this is not a predetermined fate. We don't have to allow isolation to creep up like a fog and swallow us from view. We can maintain our connections, forge new ones, and stay within sight. Like other friends of mine, I've started being proactive on a number of fronts.

I regularly assist others now—baking and sharing muffins and pies, creating their CaringBridge pages, taking on a few of their dog walks. It's not really quid pro quo—but if it works out that way, great.

I've learned there's a true sweetness to being needed and stepping up. Researchers say that every time we help another, we're rewarded with what's called a "helper's high," which is that warm, fuzzy glow you get when you've done good. I recently read a fascinating Stanford study about what's called the "kindness contagion," which refers to people imitating both the good deeds of others and the spirit underlying them. Its conclusion: "Kindness itself is contagious, and it can cascade across people, taking on new forms along the way." Count me in.

My single friends shared other ways they have of staving off the fear of being alone. "Vet out your true blues among friends, commit to them as a true blue," one posted. "Relocate to where you have friends and family," wisely noted another. Many mentioned the importance of self-care, which included a smorgasbord of ideas: don't drink too much, get regular sleep, exercise regularly, take up meditation, start new holiday traditions.

Still, all that takes effort when you wake up alone each day. I told my therapist about this fear, adding, "I feel like I'm the sole person on the planet to feel this way—even though I know that's not true." He assured me I was not the only one, then asked, "Are you talking with your friends about this?"

Thanks to his push, I started to open up to friends. Eva, a friend of more than thirty years, had lost her husband right before the holidays a couple of years earlier. She told me, "I'm trying to make new memories and new traditions in the midst of the hardest holiday season." Jill, a longtime neighbor of my parents, told me about her own anguish: "My brother died two days ago. I don't know what to do." No, of course I wasn't alone. Even in the depths of their grief, neither were Eva and Jill.

As part of my new plan, I started to initiate regular text messages and phone calls to single friends, two or three times a week. "You're not making friends sad by reminding them that they may be alone. Rather, you're reminding them that you're thinking about them. That is a great gift," said a neighbor of mine. Sometimes it's random—how can I know who needs a call most?—but sometimes I choose someone specifically. I recently texted a quick "just checking in on you" to a friend I know has been suffering from depression. His reply: "Thanks, friend. The trend is good but today is a bit of a dip so it's nice to feel your support." Two months later he reciprocated with his own call to me. Sweet.

Yes, there will always be dips—troughs, even. A few years ago, right before the holidays, a friend's Facebook post caught my eye because of the happy mother-and-daughter photo. As a caption, my friend had written: "Missing the two most loved and influential women in my life, my sister and my mother. It's my first Christmas without them both. I am trying to find the joy in the season but it would be a lie to say I am not struggling. . . . I know I'll make it, but it's harder than I thought."

I understood. Only a short time earlier, I had opened my box of Christmas ornaments and discovered the chocolate cupcake ornament and the two candy cane baubles given to me by my mother long ago. The pain of her loss hit me again like a wave.

Then I recalled a technique I learned from novelist Barbara Kingsolver about how to refind joy. "In my own worst seasons," she wrote, "I've come back from the colorless world of despair by forcing myself to look hard, for a long time, at a single glorious thing: a flame of red geranium outside my bedroom window. And then another: my daughter in a yellow dress. And another . . . until I learned to be in love with my life again."

So after hanging the ornaments, I sat and looked at the tree, with Kingsolver's resolve in mind. Gazing at the cupcake and candy cane ornaments my mother had given me, I recalled her delight in seeing me open them. The ornaments are shiny and perfect—and it turns out they are also full of memories and joy. I focused on those good feelings instead of on the pain of her loss, and I felt less alone.

Oh, and as for my colonoscopy, it all worked out. I even turned down my first volunteer. (I didn't think we were close enough friends for him to listen to me babble my way out of anesthesia or wait for me to "break wind" before being discharged.) My next-door neighbor and good friend Debbie stepped up, taking me to the clinic and waiting for me to recover. Thanks to the medications, I remember nothing about that day—except that I wasn't alone.

I Won't Let Anything Stop Me from Saying I Love You . . . and Goodbye

I won't hesitate to tell the people I care about how I feel—and when it comes time to say goodbye, I won't let my discomfort with death stop me from saying that, too.

A T THE PEAK OF THE COVID-19 pandemic I received a text from a high school friend: "Just FYI, my mother is in the hospital in NYC with a positive virus diagnosis. Not doing especially well but not unexpected at eighty-seven years old." What he meant was this: She's dying.

I asked if I could call her, since she had been best friends with my mother for a lifetime. "She's pretty weak, but I'm sure she would find talking with you heartening," he replied. One minute later I called his mother, who coughed her way through a ninety-second conversation, her lungs and airways choking with mucus, while I listened. Then I spoke. After, I texted my friend back: "I had a beautiful conversation with your mom. She said goodbye. I said goodbye. I am heartbroken for you and your sibs, but like my mother she is indelible. And will always be with us."

"I love you . . . goodbye." Not many of us want to have that talk. It's a collective denial of death, especially among the Baby Boomers who still feel immortal, sprinting and swimming like there's no tomorrow. The one thing they—um, we—can't acknowledge is that, eventually, there really is no tomorrow. (You see how hard this still is for me.)

Christopher Hitchens, the essayist and social critic, didn't shy away from having "the talk," which he described so vividly in his last book, *Mortality*, a collection of essays about dying that was published posthumously. During his brief but awful illness, Hitchens realized people need prompts on how to talk about illness and death. After what he described as a "surprisingly exhausting encounter" with a stranger who wished him well with all the wrong words, Hitchens wrote, "It made me wonder if perhaps there was room for a shorthand book of cancer etiquette" for both "sufferers" and "sympathizers."

Think about how hard it is for most of us to write a "simple" condolence note. We stammer and stall, finally put pen to paper, and then rip it all up to start again. But to confront the dying in real time, with our words and hearts . . . oh, my. I remember vividly the first time my mother acknowledged that she was dying: "Will it be painful?" she asked me. Unable to have the conversation, I pivoted to a safe topic: "What would you like for dinner tonight?"

"I don't have a whole lot of regrets in life," my longtime collaborator Roseann Henry told me, "but one of the big ones is not saying goodbye to a friend who was dying of cancer. She had stopped all treatment and was clearly approaching the end of her life, so my wife and I flew to Los Angeles for one last visit. We spent the afternoon talking about old times, current events, and the upcoming adoption of our second child. But when it came time to leave, I just couldn't bear to acknowledge the elephant in the room. All I could say was, 'Just think, next time we come back we'll have another baby with us!' We all knew we wouldn't see each other again, and in fact, the next time we went to L.A. was for her memorial service. I will always regret not saying I love you, and goodbye."

Later I told Roseann, "Sometimes we don't need words to express ourselves. No one can misinterpret the impact of showing up. You flew 2,500 miles to visit her one last time. You did say goodbye."

During my mom's lengthy illness, I closely followed NPR's Scott Simon, who tweeted his end-of-life conversations with his mother to his 2.5 million followers—one of whom was me. (He later turned this chapter of his life into a bestselling memoir, *Unforgettable: A Son, a Mother, and the Lessons of a Lifetime,* which is both a love story and a how-to manual for saying goodbye in the digital age.) Simon stayed at his mother's bedside—sometimes *in* her hospital bed—comforting her, having frank conversations, until the end. In a phone conversation, Simon told me, "A gentleman always sees a lady to the door"—in this case, her final door. This is one of the lessons he says his mother taught him.

"I understand there are people who think they can't bring themselves to do it," he added, "but it becomes an utterly natural thing. My mother said to me at one point, 'Will this go on forever?' I said, 'No, it won't go on forever.' She said, 'You and me, we'll go on forever?' I just said, 'Yes.'"

But how do you know when to have this talk, especially when we're holding on to the last flicker of hope? If a loved one has a protracted illness, having the conversation too soon could be awkward—if not downright ghoulish. Too late, however—well, that's a bigger problem. Even though I couldn't acknowledge it at the time, my mom opened the door for me when she asked, "Will dying be painful?" Fortunately, in the weeks that she had left, I found myself able to step through the open door to be with her.

Crossing that threshold is a gift, albeit a painful one. Only a few days ago as I write this, I visited the Caring-Bridge website of my friend and ex-partner, Barry Owen, who had been diagnosed with Stage IV pancreatic cancer twelve months earlier. Now, he'd terminated treatment and was nearing the end of his life. Many of his dear friends openly expressed their love and their sadness at the impending loss. One of them posted, "I have seen deaths both sudden and drawn-out. To my mind, if you can have some time when you KNOW FOR SURE you are

dying but you are still in a state of consciousness to ap-
preciate your loved ones, say what needs to be said, and
then orient your heart and mind and spirit to the transi-
tion, that is a truly wonderful gift. So many people are
denied that special time. I am so glad Barry and Dan [his
husband] have this last phase together: holding you both
deeply in my heart." The rest of us, several dozen, hit the
"love" icon to say, "I agree!"

In my last email to Barry, I'd written, "Let me close
with this for now. I'm sure you remember my landlord-
turned-friend Denise. About the time she turned ninety,
we began ending all of your conversations with 'I love
you.' We continued that until she was ninety-eight, and
two weeks before she died, we signed off on the phone
with that mantra. 'I love you, Barry.' I hope to write that
to you for eight more years." Barry died three months
later.

Actually, when it came to Denise, I have to admit I
erred on the early side—by nearly a full decade. When
she turned ninety in 2007, we both understood she'd entered "double overtime" (as she put it). She no longer
lived in the San Francisco flat where I'd once been her
tenant; she'd recently moved to a continuing care facility just across from the Golden Gate Bridge. On a long
flight from the East Coast, I wrote Denise my goodbye
letter. Just penning it brought back so many wonderful
memories, like this one: For twenty-five years, we had
our own secret monikers (like agents 86 and 99 on the
classic TV show *Get Smart*). I called Denise "621," and she
referred to me as "548"—our phone exchanges when we

first met. We'd always greet each other this way, pretending no one else knew our silly code names.

The afternoon of my visit, Denise made us some tea in her one-bedroom apartment and tore open a Trader Joe's chocolate bar for us to share. We chatted for a while before I took out my letter, which I then read aloud to her.

> Dear Denise,
>
> I'm on the plane and reading Armistead Maupin's *Michael Tolliver Lives* from the *Tales of the City* saga. I've always thought you reminded me of the landlady, Anna Madrigal of Barbary Lane, and I've always been, in my mind, Michael Tolliver to you. Anna is approaching her late eighties in this book, and she tells Michael how much he has meant to her. He chokes up. Moments later, he says: "I should have reciprocated and told her everything she'd meant to me, but I couldn't. It would have been too official somehow, too final. I told myself there would be other times, better opportunities, that it didn't really have to be here and now."
>
> Like Michael, I've wanted to tell you everything you mean to me without sounding "too official, too final." How to start?
>
> Two years ago, when I was deciding whether or not to move to North Carolina, I knew I had the gift of time to return to the Bay Area if it didn't work out. But, and this was a big but, I also knew that despite your amazing longevity,

you would not live forever, and that time has a way of shutting down a hand—or a life—Boom! Bye-bye.

Of course, you endorsed my adventure, because you are an adventuress yourself! You taught me that life never stays the same, and that we need to stay open to the currents and shifts that shake our foundations. That is just one of the reasons I love you.

Here's another: When we first met, you were seventy-seven and copyediting the community paper, taking water aerobics, and being "another grandmother for peace."

What a role model, I thought.

The two years I spent living in the flat underneath yours—hearing your pitter-pat above me—will always be among the happiest in my life. I can only call it by its name: magical.

Since then, I've watched you grow and struggle, and have seen the texture of your emotional life deepen (not always without pain). Others might have decided it was time to coast, but not you, my dear. I try to emulate that—to never rest in the static but dig in my roots, deep and wide, even when it's scary or hurts. Thank you for that.

So, how to tell you what you mean to me? I can't possibly. Suffice to say that your love and wisdom, your lightheartedness and frivolity, your passions and convictions, mean so much. I

feel like I've known you my whole life and I
know that I will love you, remember you, rejoice
in you, and eat chocolate with you for all our
days to come . . . and beyond.

Love, Steven

Once I'd finished, Denise kissed me on the cheek, told
me how much she loved me, and poured us another cup
of tea.

As it turned out, we had each other for years to come.
Toward the end of her life, when she had trouble recognizing my voice on the phone, I'd shout into the receiver:
"621, it's 548!" That did the trick; we were secret agents
again—and forever.

When it finally came time to say goodbye to my
mother a few years later, I'd had some practice. For the
three years of Mom's illness, I'd told her "I love you" every
time we hung up the phone or said goodbye in person. As
that last Christmas approached, Mom's death was imminent. As her holiday gift, she'd asked all three of her kids
to visit together. She didn't say "one last time," but we
knew that's what she meant. My sister was overseas, so
we planned to meet at our parents' apartment right after
the New Year.

On a snowy evening in early January 2017, my brother,
sister, and I all came to see Mom, squeezing into the tiny
apartment. Once she knew we were there, Mom slipped
into unconsciousness, the state doctors call "unresponsive." My sister Julie swears she saw Mom tear up when
she said her final goodbye. As for me, I held Mom's hands

and told her repeatedly "I love you, Mommy," just as I had as a child. Soon after midnight, with the snow coming down hard outside her bedroom window, our mother died, surrounded by love. I had no regrets.

I Won't Postpone
for Tomorrow What
Matters to Me Today

Dreaming about the future may be diverting enough when we're young, with the days of our lives still ahead of us. But as the years tick by and we realize we're running out of time, it becomes more important than ever to seize the day.

HO KNOWS WHEN the bell will toll for me? Or any of us?

That was my frame of mind on the day I visited DeathClock.com, the Internet's "friendly"—although not entirely scientific—"reminder that life is slipping away . . . second by second." After I completed the short questionnaire, the Death Clock's algorithm quickly did the math, spitting out its calculation: "Your personal day of death is Wednesday, April 23, 2031." If correct, I will be seventy-three years old on that day.

Not happy with this result, I queried my oncologist about my expected longevity. He quickly emailed back:

"All things being equal, I believe your estimated survival time would be around 72 to 75. Good luck."

Good luck? I spent a few moments processing the possible meanings behind that phrase, letting it sink in that my well-trained doc had basically corroborated the Death Clock's calculation. For a few moments I sat there feeling sorry for myself, imagining the hourglass emptying. Then, not allowing myself to wallow one grain of sand longer, I decided to quit my day job.

Yes, just like that. Call me crazy, irrational, impetuous—or all three. For decades, I'd worked as a salaried editor. Ironically, my soon-to-be-former boss once gave me a copy of Malcolm Gladwell's *Blink: The Power of Thinking Without Thinking,* telling me point-blank, "You need to learn to put more trust in your impulses." I had underlined this particular section: "Decisions made very quickly can be every bit as good as decisions made cautiously and deliberately."

I'd long fantasized about quitting my job. But so many fears had stood in my way, starting with the most basic: dollars and cents. Yes, I had already downsized by moving to a smaller and less-expensive house. Yes, I'd been squirreling away a rainy-day fund. And yes—and most significantly—I'd been talking regularly with my therapist not just about quitting, but about how to live a truly meaningful life. "But is it already too late?" I asked him. No, he replied, and then quoted the novelist and feminist Margaret Deland: "As soon as you feel too old to do a thing, do it."

I did not want to become one of those awful mortality statistics. Retirement, especially for men, is a real killer.

A recent study found that those who retired at age fifty-five were nearly 90 percent more likely to die in the following decade than those who retired at sixty-five. I felt certain those early retirees were already sick or had unhealthy lifestyles. But I was wrong. "There is . . . reason to believe retirement in general could cause you to meet your maker sooner than intended," which is how The *Wall Street Journal* reported on the study.

This "Retirement Equals Death" connection slaps me in the face every time I read about famous folks who take possession of their gold watches and promptly bite the dust. Take Frank Deford, the longtime sports writer and NPR commentator. On May 3, 2017, Deford, 78, signed off with his last weekly public radio commentary—number 1,656—and by the end of the month, he was dead. College football coach Paul William "Bear" Bryant died in 1983, at age 69, just thirty-seven days after coaching his last game. Charles M. Schulz, 77, who created the Charlie Brown and Snoopy characters (among many other be-loveds), announced his retirement in November 1999 and died not even two months later—the day after the final *Peanuts* strip ran in newspapers

Thanks to the Death Clock, deciding to leave my job was a Gladwell no-brainer, but I wasn't intending to retire.

I didn't plan to spend the rest of my life traveling the world. First of all, my rainy-day fund isn't that big. And as near as my time horizon may have sounded, that was still a heck of a lot of days and weeks not to fritter away. Rather, my plan was to do full time what I loved, what I'd been doing in bits and pieces, in between jobs, on vacations, before the workday and after hours: write.

Fortunately, I had some role models in making this leap. My friend Peter, then fifty-three, a documentarian, had left his full-time job eighteen months earlier to take what he called "a sabbatical" to write a play. He explained to me, "I realized it was a myth to think there would be a time when I don't have any financial worries. If not now, when?" One of his closest friends had recently died of a malignant brain tumor at age fifty-two. "That was a very real accelerator of my decision."

Similarly, my neighbor Tom, exactly my age, told me over coffee he'd come to a realization: "I only have so many years left." A photographer and writer, he'd recently stepped down from a university directorship after watching two of his closest friends pass away—"guys that I thought were bulletproof," he explained. "I want to quit talking about doing my own work—and *do* my own work."

The week after getting my doctor's "good luck" email, I gave notice. I told a good story, but what I didn't say was this: "I've got only one life to live, and if I don't do it now, when?" I was fifty-six.

I couldn't sleep the next few nights, the loud echoes of my naysayers circling through my head. But over the weeks that followed, things began to shift. I started to get new assignments and finished up a book proposal. I'd get up at 5 a.m. as excited as a kid on Christmas morning. I felt a new sense of ownership, joy, and meaning to my days. This wasn't my work, it was my life. And I didn't just like it—I loved it.

Of course, I'm not living in a state of 24/7 euphoria. I struggle with everything from blank pages to intermittent paychecks to moments of self-doubt about my decision (especially when the stock market tumbles). My *annus horribilis* came not long after; that was the year both my parents died and my husband left me. I was on my own in every way.

Still, I regularly turn to a few lines of a novel by Wendell Berry that my friend Tom passed along: "Back at the beginning, as I see now, my life was all time and almost no memory. . . . And now, nearing the end, I see that my life is almost entirely memory and very little time."

No, I won't postpone for tomorrow what I care about today.

I Won't Let Anyone
Else Write My Obituary

Call me a control freak, but when it comes time to write the final summary of my life, I know I am the best one to do it. So hands off my obit!

IKE ME, MY DAD LEFT LITTLE to chance, including his obituary. Ten years before he died, he handed me a manila folder that contained a photocopy of his résumé as well as a few other notes for his final story. He even told me the three newspapers where he wanted it published. He had achieved many professional accolades, but I knew—because he told me—nothing was more important to him than the decades he spent teaching at NYU. Here's how he wrote it: "NYU recognized his excellence as an educator when they presented him with a Golden Dozen award for his exceptional teaching."

I wondered whether leaving such exacting guidance was a rare human quirk, and so I began asking friends if any of them had pre-written their own obituaries. Aha! I was surprised to learn how many already had. Bryce, in his mid-fifties, raised his hand first: "I have! Control freak to the end." When I asked him why he felt this was necessary, he answered, "My parents and brother aren't great writers. Plus, there are things about my life I want included. I would love to say it's to save them the trouble, but my motives are more narcissistic."

Motives aside, Bryce wasn't the only one who attributed this to a controlling impulse (one said she's considered writing hers "just so it would be grammatically correct"). Many people confessed to pure ego: They'd not only written their own obits but also regularly updated them with their latest accomplishments.

"There's a feminist argument for writing your own," my friend Ellen explained. "Women so often get overlooked in regards to their accomplishments outside the domestic sphere." (Yes, just look at the new-ish *Times* series of obits on "overlooked women.") Ronny, a banker in her sixties, explained her motives: "I wrote my obituary over four decades ago. Little did I know it would be the start of a journey I wouldn't have missed for the world. . . . Where my résumé listed the jobs I held, my obituary would chronicle the importance of public service, the opportunities opened by being an entrepreneur, and the personal satisfaction of philanthropy."

One of my college mentors, Gloria Emerson, the first female *New York Times* writer to report from Vietnam, was exacting about language to the very end. Not long before her suicide in 2004, "Miss Emerson," as she was known formally, left a carefully composed obituary, typed out on her house stationery with a handful of corrections made in her own script. Before taking her life, she mailed it to a *Times* colleague, with instructions to make sure it was not assigned to a particular book critic—one who had written "a savage review of [her] book *Winners & Losers*" some twenty-five years earlier. Her final wish: "Please do the obit for me." He did. (And it was printed word for word as Miss Emerson had typed it.)

Not a writer? No worries—today, you can hire one. My friend Daniel Wallace, a well-known writer, once started a personalized service for death notices called "To Die For Obits," which allowed you "to write the obituary you'd want, not the one others would want for you." The price? $2,500, with 50 percent down on signing and the remainder on fulfillment. (Alas, Daniel's business died, but there are plenty of other obit writing services on the web.) All in all, a reminder that death is not cheap, and that future planning helps our heirs save time and money.

I've always said to myself, "You need to know how a story ends before you can understand its meaning." To be honest, on this vow, I'm not there yet. But like my dad, I keep my résumé all up to date, except that it's stored on LinkedIn and not a Xerox photocopy in a manila folder. I hope I'll get to the rest before The End gets to me.

I Won't Forget to Plan My Own Funeral

I know exactly what kind of send-off I would like, and I've already started making plans for it—unlike my parents, who had to be strong-armed into giving me their final answer for their final resting place.

AS A GIFT MANY YEARS AGO, an eminently practical and thrifty cousin presented our family with funeral plots in a windswept Cape Cod cemetery—five of them, sufficient for Mom and Dad, my two siblings, and me. As Cousin Nina told my father, "They were cheaper by the dozen," so she had purchased not just five but twelve, giving the rest to other cousins. Nina, to round out my portrait of this quirky relative, had given me a crocheted toilet cozy—that's a matching tank and seat cover set—when I turned eleven.

The consummate planner, Nina was an outlier in our family, since my folks were hardly known for looking ahead, much less dwelling on final dispositions. In fact, my journalist father, who harangued me when growing up about the proper use of tenses, especially the subjunctive, would later in life preface any mention of his own passing with "*If* I die . . ." to which I had the satisfaction of responding that this was no time for the subjunctive. "Dad, it's *when*, not *if*."

But it wasn't just denial that stood in the way of our choosing a final resting place. My parents also had very little tradition to build on. My maternal grandparents had been buried deep in a Queens, New York, mausoleum that I've never visited; I can't even tell you the name of the cemetery. Grandma Marian, on my dad's side, buried her husband under one of his prize rosebushes in the backyard of a house now owned by God knows whom. As for Marian herself, she made sure her body was dispatched to New York University to train a new generation of medical students.

On this subject, I am a very different beast than the rest of my family. Perhaps because I'd been given a cancer diagnosis early in life, or because I'd lost so many friends in the AIDS epidemic, or maybe just because I'm an obsessive-compulsive planner, I long ago labeled a manila folder "Notes for SP Funeral/Memorial." Among the bits and pieces in that now worn folder is a program from a friend's wedding at San Francisco's Swedenborgian Church. Its warm interior features massive timbers of Pacific madrone and high wainscoting of Douglas fir. I want to make sure my funeral is held there. There's also a neon-pink Post-it in the folder that reads, "Play *The Mary Tyler Moore Show* theme song, 'Love Is All Around,' at some point in the service," which will surprise no one who knows me well.

Oh, and there's a photograph of the Arlington National Cemetery grave markers for President and Mrs. Kennedy, specifying that my stone be from the same Massachusetts quarry with the same typeface. Yes, I'm an outlier, but this will also make the necessary arrangements so much easier for my next of kin.

By age thirty-five, I had planned my final party. The location of my after-party, however, where I'd rest for eternity, remained as opaque as my parents'. We'd turned down Nina's gift, but I had nowhere else in mind as a final resting place.

A decade later, I found myself visiting Sag Harbor, New York, an old whaling village near where our family vacationed and where I have happy childhood memories of Fourth of July parades, strawberry shortcake, and summer clambakes. By happenstance, one August evening I drove past Oakland Cemetery, an oasis lovingly conjured by so many writers and one local poet who noted the "filtered sunlight" and "sighing winds."

I stopped and got out of the car. Walking the grounds, I discovered many notables lay six feet under: the choreographer George Balanchine, two Iranian princes, and Revolutionary War hero David Hand (buried along with his five wives). A massive boulder listed the names of five men, lifelong friends, who had died from HIV/AIDS by the early 1990s. (They had been cremated and then buried together beneath the stone.)

I put in a call to ask about the availability of plots, and a Mr. Yardley said they still had some in the original burial ground—although, like everyone in the Hamptons, they were "adding on."

I told my parents about Oakland Cemetery and we scheduled a visit; they canceled. ("We need to take the dog to the vet.") We rescheduled; they canceled again. ("Oh no, we're double booked.") On the fourth try, we made it out there: Mom, Dad, my sister Julie, Julie's wife, and me. (My brother and his wife didn't want any part of this real estate deal. I guess they will remain homeless in the afterlife.)

In the dead of winter, Mr. Yardley walked us to a site where, lo and behold, we could have six contiguous plots for $600 apiece—cheaper by the half-dozen, in this case— surely the best real estate deal on the East End.

Mom, who had been complaining that her feet were "frostbitten," was willing to say yes if it got us closer to lunch and a gin gimlet. I could see Dad was ambivalent, not as much about the graveyard as about dying. As was customary for him, he took off to wander a bit, heading down toward the new "development." Ten minutes later, he returned and said: "Okay, we'll do it. I saw Clay Felker's grave marker over there. This is a good 'hood for me." Dad was satisfied enough to become a permanent resident at Oakland Cemetery if it meant being in the company of the founder and editor of *New York* magazine.

And so we agreed to buy all six plots, with one to spare. My mom especially liked the notion that we'd all be together again—eventually.

Now another decade has come and gone, and my parents are buried at Oakland Cemetery. Next to Dad's

"Professor and Journalist" marker is Mom's "Beloved By All" stone, with a towering oak between them. As for the rest of us, we're still here, not there, with the deed safely in my manila folder. We all have a shady place to call home for eternity.

I Won't Die Without Writing Letters to My Loved Ones

———

A final message to family and friends, delivered after my death, will be my personal way of thanking those who meant the most to me and saying goodbye to them. Now . . . when to start writing them?

M Y SISTER AND I HAD just ordered lunch at a bright new restaurant in downtown Houston when she started to cry. This was just a few weeks after she learned of a recurrence of the ovarian cancer she'd been diagnosed with the year before. It was a few days before Christmas 2018, and we had traveled to MD Anderson Cancer Center seeking a second opinion. In those intervening weeks, we'd talked with her doctors at Memorial Sloan Kettering, a team at Dana-Farber, and a solo researcher in the Bronx. For the first time in those weeks, we found a moment just to *be*.

That's when Julie started to cry, for the first time since getting the news. "Do you think it's time for me to write letters to the girls?" she asked, referring to her two daughters (my nieces), Jessie and Caroline.

I knew the kind of letters she meant. Only a few years earlier, my college friend Jacqueline Zinn had been diagnosed with a brain tumor. After eighteen months of treatment, Jacquie (as she was known) passed away at age fifty-six, leaving behind a husband and four kids. The letters she left behind were thoughtful, touching, and memorable.

Jacquie and I had been classmates at Duke University in the '70s and became friends again in the 2000s. We spent most Saturday mornings together at a Spin class, competing against each other as though we were sister and brother racing to avoid the dreaded middle seat on a long car ride. A triathlete, Jacquie beat me nine times out of ten and always left the class on a high note, exclaiming, "That was fabulous!" She wasn't lauding her victories, but the very endorphin-filled experience itself.

Then one winter's day, when we were both planning to attend our ninety-one-year-old friend Mary's funeral at Duke University Chapel, Jacquie absented herself. Less than a mile away, at Duke University Hospital, she found herself face-to-face with a diagnosis of glioblastoma, the nastiest of brain cancers. Despite the grim prognosis, Jacquie, then fifty-five, left no stone unturned in seeking a cure.

Over the months, I watched as Jacquie succeeded in achieving remission and returned to Spin. A few months later, though, the cancer returned, this time with a greater vengeance. Jacquie was into the second year of her illness when she (along with her husband Doug) came to understand that the cancer would claim her life. Jacquie asked her oncologist how long she had to live. He said, "I can't tell you. No one can ever know." She pressed him further: "Weeks or months?" "Weeks," he replied.

When Doug recounted that conversation, I thought: How many of us could ever ask such a question?

It's what happened next, however, that I found truly extraordinary. In facing her impending death, Jacquie transformed what was already a profile in courage to a tale of determination I'd not personally witnessed before.

As Doug explained to me a month after his wife died, "Once she understood the road ahead of her, she took charge of her future. She canceled her credit cards, gave her clothes to her sisters, and she taught me how to pay our bills."

Once those tasks were done, Jacquie, who had long been a project manager at GlaxoSmithKline, undertook her final effort. As Doug put it, "Her end of life experience was project managing her funeral." In a series of meetings with her priest, Jacquie planned her own service, choosing her favorite reflections, readings, and hymns.

As I thumbed through the program at her service, I came to an insert called "In Gratitude." The broadside began by giving thanks to Jacquie's many caregivers. It was written in the first person, and I assumed that Doug, an accomplished writer himself, was its author. That is, until it suddenly became evident that the author's "I" was, in fact, Jacquie herself.

In her valedictory to the rest of us, she ended with these lines: "I had a blessed and wonderful life. Of course I would still love to be with you on earth, but that was not God's plan for me. I tried my hardest to beat this illness, but things are not always under our control. I hope I am now with my Heavenly Father and my dad, watching over all of you."

By this time, I was in tears, as was just about everyone else reading these words—so full of life and joy, promise and preparation. Still, Jacquie had one last admonition to those of us gathered in her honor that steamy July day: "Please go out and celebrate my life. It was fabulous!!"

But it was hearing about another end-of-life project that moved me even more. "Every night for weeks, she wrote letters to our children," Doug recalled. Jacquie wrote multiple letters to each child, to be opened at different life milestones. Jacquie wanted to be "present with her kids," Doug explained, at each of those important moments: graduations, marriages, the births of what would have been her grandkids.

Several years after Doug told me about the letters, in the wake of both my parents' deaths and when I started working on this book, I reached out to Jacquie's second-born son, Jerry, who was writing about the loss of his mother. I asked if he'd be willing to share those letters with me. Doug had already given him two—one soon after Jacquie's death and the other when Jerry graduated from college. Jerry will receive his next letter when he marries.

After some hesitation, mostly about what his mother would have counseled, he agreed, hoping that their publication would help to keep Jacquie's memory alive.

"The letters my mother left me are among the most precious gifts I possess," he told me. "She diligently took the time, the very limited time, as her life was coming to an end to sit down and think about her children's futures."

One day, in perfect cursive penmanship and blue ink, a month before her death, Jacquie wrote her first letter to Jerry, then age nineteen.

> Dear Jerry, my budding film-maker,
>
> I know you have a lot of emotions running through you, as I did when my father died, but I was much older than you at the time, so I really can't begin to truly comprehend what you are feeling. I am so incredibly sorry that I had to die while you are so young and I assume it sucks for you. Perhaps you can use some of these emotions and feelings in your upcoming work(s), assuming you continue to pursue film.
>
> Let me assure you that I did absolutely everything I could to stay alive for as long as possible. I know you realize that having been with me at many of my treatments or tests. Plus the acupuncture, tons of praying I also did. But for some reason I just didn't make it as one of the chosen ones to be cured. But because of what I did I'm sure I lived much longer than if I hadn't been in good shape to begin with.

I am incredibly proud of you for everything you have done in your relatively short life. I will be watching over you every day to see what new and exciting things you will accomplish— regardless of what occupations(s) you pursue over your lifetime.

Do your best to support Dad and your siblings, especially during this first year as it will be the hardest for everyone. I remember that from when my father died. Time will certainly help, but it takes a long time to focus on the happy memories while the sad thoughts are more immediate and closer at hand.

I had many fantastic years on earth, more than a lot of people, hence, I have no complaints. I survived a melanoma, car accident in the mountains of West Virginia with Uncle Jerry, car accident in Durham. So I have already lived many lives and I was extremely grateful for each and every moment. Try and live your life that way and you will be a happy and fulfilled human being.

I love more than you will ever know, my dearest Jerry.

Love, Mom

Three years later, on the day Jerry graduated from the University of North Carolina at Chapel Hill in 2016, Doug handed over letter number two, written with the same pen, on the same type of notepaper.

My sweet dear Jerry,

Well—this is it—a big milestone in your life—college graduation! Congratulations. I am so incredibly proud of you no matter what your major or minors. I know you made it worthwhile and got just exactly what you wanted to out of the experience. I know you learned an incredible amount about subjects and probably an even greater amount about people.

Jacquie signs off with these words:

I am watching over you all the time, or at least I hope I can do that! Congratulations, again. Enjoy this fabulous day and all the celebrations around. Big Hugs and Kisses!

Much Love, Mom

Jerry said that at various times during college he had considered dropping out, but "knowing that I would never receive that letter if I did not graduate was a very strong influence in keeping me in school. The letter was a motivation for which I will be forever grateful." Knowing Jacquie as I did, I'm certain that was part of her master plan.

What a gift, an eternal gift, I thought as I read and reread the two letters. I silently bowed in amazement, remembering that Doug told me that she'd written all these letters while in a wheelchair, paralyzed on one side.

I knew it was time for me to get my act together and face my own excursion into the afterlife. I needed to rewrite my will, since I was now legally separated, and update my medical power of attorney. Yet every time I considered reading over the documents I found myself crashing head-on into the wall of denial. Finally, my attorney begged me to at least acknowledge that I was receiving her emails, even if I wouldn't respond to them. "Yes," I replied tersely. All this resistance—and I wasn't suffering from any serious, much less terminal, condition.

Yet with Jacquie's example in mind, I finally sat down and read the pile of documents. To my surprise, I found comfort in taking care of that necessary business—once it was done, anyway. I'd like to think that was something Jacquie felt, too, as she sent her missives into the future.

I have taken mental inventory of the people who should get letters from me after I'm gone, but I haven't started writing them yet. I know that to get started is to admit that I'm approaching "The End." Fortunately, I'm still here—not there.

As for my sister, Julie, no letters needed. Her current treatment plan is keeping the disease at bay.

I Won't Be
Disappointed by My Life

We are only given a limited number of decades in our lives—it would be a terrible thing to come to their end with a sense of disappointment. I am in charge of how my life turns out, and I will make the most of it.

I WAS SITTING WITH MY DAD one late winter day when he asked me out of the blue, "What matters in life to you?"

The question startled me, especially since I knew Dad didn't have any spiritual, much less religious, beliefs. My off-the-cuff answer rambled, but I know it included my husband (at the time), my brother and sister, our family more broadly, the many friends I've cultivated over a lifetime, my work—and, yes, my health. I then asked him the same question. He sat in his wicker chair staring out the window, seemingly for an eternity. When he returned his gaze to me, he simply shrugged his shoulders. No words. My heart broke for him.

Not long after that "conversation," Dad published a book titled *Very Short Fictions*, with a long and unwieldy subtitle: "Tales of friendship, romance, sex, love, romantic dissolutions, business and professional affairs, family matters, historical memories, illness, loss, and other aspects of everyday life and death in its full and unpredictable variety."

A mere fifty-nine pages, the slim volume gave voice to that shoulder shrug. In it, he wrote about the disappointments of his long life. Oh, and it was far from fiction, more closely resembling a memoir. In describing the lifelong chasm between two of his "fictional" characters—father and son—in a chapter titled "Different Planets," Dad penned: "His son was gay, and he was not, and even though their relationship was correct, cordial, even friendly, it lacked intimacy; they had lived such different lives." That didn't sound much like fiction to me, his gay son.

Unfortunately, my relationship with my father was never as close or comfortable as the one I came to share with my mom. Dad was a variant of the archetypical 1950s father: He kept his feelings pretty much to himself. He worked long hours as a journalist and traveled a good deal to cover breaking stories like JFK's assassination and the rocket launches from Cape Canaveral. He had a reporter's keen ability to ask questions—dozens of them, often very intrusive ones—but less capacity to reciprocate with answers of his own.

Many of his book's chapters focused on my mother and their marriage of sixty-three years.

MORNING MEMORIES

On awakening, his wife told him that she remembers being very angry at him the night before but couldn't remember why; he remembered why but didn't tell her.

HOW IT STARTED

One evening, walking side by side towards Third Avenue, he felt her press her breast into his shoulder, and keep it there.

A MARRIAGE

As they entered their 60s, they started bickering; the culmination of decades of marriage.

I understood how he might have been disappointed. Like me, Dad was better at expressing himself in print. When I read *Very Short Fictions*, I learned even more. If one theme prevailed, it was a bittersweet—often sour—remembrance of things past.

THE DREAMER

When he thinks of all the lives he could have lived, he thinks of being a Frenchman living in Lyons, or an Argentinean on the Pampas; then he goes to work in downtown Brooklyn.

SURF'S UP

There came the day when, with the surf heavy, he could no longer swim through the breakers to the sand bar beyond. His two teen-age sons could do so easily.

SIGNS OF AGING

He knew he was getting older when it took him longer to do what he used to do easily, and quickly, so he decided to do less, but even that took longer.

ANOTHER SIGN OF AGING

He knew he was getting older when his children started telling him what to do, not the other way round, as it should be.

ACADEMIC POLITICS

The senior professor told his wife that the new chairman had talked about getting rid of "dead wood"; that evening he had trouble getting to sleep.

TOO LATE

At family gatherings, he grew uneasy when his adult children talked about their childhood; invariably they remembered events he wished he had handled differently.

To understand my father better required some triangulation. Ironically, after his death and after reading the many eulogies written in his honor, I had a more complete—but still not full—picture of him.

Here are some of the tributes posted on his "In Memoriam" website.

Bill Moyers, public broadcasting documentarian (Dad produced the eleven-part PBS documentary *In Search of the Constitution*, among other Moyers programs):

> When they invented the word "stalwart," the gods of language surely had Dick Petrow in mind. He was a resolute and loyal colleague, a stout ally as deadlines loomed, a script floundered, a conundrum taunted, or a picture wouldn't stay locked.

Dan Barry, reporter and columnist for *The New York Times*:

> Dick Petrow was my news writing professor during my first year as a graduate student at NYU's department of journalism. He broke me of my undergraduate tendency to muse and to opine and to write about the world in the precious first person. He taught me how to report hard news; how to write clearly on deadline; how to cut out the nonsense. In other words, how to be a newspaper reporter.

Rakisha Kearns-White, a 1994 NYU journalism graduate and now a librarian:

> Nearly twenty-five years later, Professor Petrow is one of a handful of NYU professors whose

> name I still remember. . . . Every time I write an
> email or a grant proposal, I remember the les-
> sons I learned about writing with concise clarity
> and without clichés. Professor Petrow is still a
> genuine influence on my life.

I know Dad would have especially liked Rakisha's tribute because she clearly had learned his two most
important lessons: (1) Write with clarity and without
clichés. (2) Call him Professor Petrow.

With praise and accolades from admirers like these,
how could Dad still have been so disappointed with his
life? Why did I learn more about him in the fifty-nine
pages of his book than I had by being his son? My siblings
and I recognized ourselves and our family in his stories,
which rang true no matter how painful they were to read.

As his disability grew and his fears deepened, he
didn't share his haunting thoughts with any of us, but he
continued to write about the slights, shunnings, and a
world growing ever smaller.

Among the forty-odd stories, this is the one that
pained me the most:

WHILE DRIVING

All his life he drove a black four-door family
sedan but when motorcyclists roared past him
on his left, he felt that life had passed him by as
well.

While he may have felt that way at the end, I don't think Dad would want me to end there. Nor do I. Here's what I wrote on his NYU tribute site:

> I owe many things to my father, and a career in journalism is one of them. As determined as I was to do things my own way, by midlife I realized that was not entirely the case. I must have inherited the "journalism" gene as, like my dad, I've wandered the country as a reporter, spent years writing books in near solitude, and enjoyed just about every minute of this wild and crazy ride. Thanks, Dad.

Afterword

WHAT A DIFFERENCE A DECADE can make. For my fiftieth birthday, my parents hosted a New England clambake at their beach house: lobster and steamer clams, local mussels and summer sweet corn on the cob, my mom's most mayonnaise-y potato salad, and lots and lots of bib napkins. Oh, for dessert, my favorite: an eight-layered strawberry shortcake. Twenty-five of my closest friends flew in from all over the country to help celebrate me, sleeping in every bed (and on the floor) and at various neighbors' homes. The evening was beyond lovely, and my parents proved generous in every way. My mother had long joked, quoting one of Phyllis Diller's famous zingers, "I want my children to have all the things I couldn't afford. Then I want to move in with them." She was paying it backward.

When the celebration came to an end, Dad explained how happy he was to have had the gathering—but he also told me, "That's the last big party we're hosting. It was too exhausting." He kept his word.

By the time my sixtieth birthday rolled around, both he and my mom had passed. At that year's birthday dinner (a much smaller gathering in a restaurant), my siblings and I toasted the memory of our parents, putting aside much of the *Sturm und Drang* of their final decade. My sister remarked, "They'd have enjoyed the evening—especially having no official duties." And I quipped, "Mom would have asked me how old I was, and then when I answered, she'd have mocked a scream: 'How can I be the mother of a sixty-year-old?'" And we would have laughed at that—just as we had when she'd asked the same question when I turned forty, and then fifty.

Julie, Jay, and I had done our flawed best in taking care of our parents—and we were coming to believe that our parents had also done their flawed best in crossing the threshold from midlife to old, and then to sick.

On the evening of my sixtieth, it proved challenging not to think about "then" and "now," and I thought about that decade a lot as I wrote this book. I had started out with that snarky, highly judgmental list, but I ended up with a different—dare I say, more compassionate—perspective on them and what it means to get older.

I still want to make different choices than they did. In fact, I've already started. Not too long ago, I found myself trying to grab a book off the top shelf—my left foot on a chair, my right on my desk. With one hand, I held onto the bookshelf, and then I jumped up—just for a second—to snatch the book. In that moment, I said to myself, "This is not a good idea anymore." And I vowed to get the stepladder the next time. With a nod to Neil Armstrong, the first man to land on the moon, "That's one small step for me, one giant leap in coming to terms with an uncertain future."

But I also understand better now why my parents and their generation did things the way they did. I only have to think back to my grandparents—their parents—to see their long shadow cast over Mom and Dad. One lesson learned: We're all imprints of those who came before us.

A second lesson: I don't see my parents' behaviors and attitudes now as "wrong" (much less "stupid") so much as self-defeating. I wanted more for them—more travel to see their friends and the world, more inclusion in our daily lives, more autonomy, and above all, more happiness and less worry. Many of their choices narrowed their lives, and may have shortened their days. With hindsight, I think that around the time of my clambake birthday, as they edged upward from seventy-five, they'd embarked on a long slumber. Each passing year brought diminished awareness of the consequences of their choices.

"It is utterly false and cruelly arbitrary to put all the play and learning into childhood, all the work into middle age, and all the regrets into old age," Margaret Mead once perceptively wrote. That's what I saw happening with my parents—and so many others of their generation. My anger and obstinacy, when it came to Mom and Dad's choices, masked my sadness and my fear of my own gene pool.

Let me return to Jimmy Carter once again, who is among my top role models for "old." In his book *The Virtues of Aging*, he quotes a friend's advice: "We worry too much about something to live on—and too little about something to live for." In other words, what point is there in a life without goals or purpose, or in which we stagnate, if not atrophy? Waiting for the other shoe to drop is not the purpose I had in mind for my parents—or for me—in this last set of chapters.

Lesson number three: With hindsight, I wish I'd been less of a "know-it-all" with Dad, giving him more space to say yes, rather than his reflexive no, which I knew all too well. With Mom, I'm still chagrined that I was a quick draw to anger and frustration.

Until I turned sixty, I didn't feel ready to start taking my own advice; I was still busily adding to my list, not implementing it. But that's changed. I've had my hearing checked. I (mostly) take my medications as prescribed. I've made progress on Marie Kondo-ing my house—leaving much less for someone else to dispose of when the time comes.

Unfortunately, in recent years I've watched close friends, colleagues, and celebrities die prematurely, either suddenly or after long illnesses, without even having had the chance to become "old." When the pioneering sportscaster and former Miss America Phyllis George died at age seventy, my college friend Laura Ann, one month younger than me, texted me: "That proves we're old."

"No," I quickly replied. "Her premature death proves she was ill—she had this cancer in some form for thirty-five years." Another lesson remembered: Growing old is not the same as growing ill, and I am grateful for the opportunity to age in good health, for as long as that lasts.

Every so often, I turn back to my list of "stupid things" to help me remember, to keep me on track. I'm doing my level best—flawed though that may be—to make smarter choices. But these days I laugh at myself—and kind of cringe—when I recognize Mom or Dad in my actions or reactions (which I do more often that I'd care to admit). Is it genetics? Can it be overcome? A friend reminds me, "The important thing is to remember no matter how much we tell ourselves we won't be like our parents, no matter how hard and fast we run in the other direction, we become them." Please, say it's not so!

I'm also trying hard not to inhale all those negative stereotypes about aging and old people as destiny. I'm looking to new role models. Take Jane Fonda, now well into her eighties and continuing to work as an actor and activist, who told a reporter, "I believe that your mind can overcome a lot of the failings of your body as you get older by maintaining a youthful spirit and a passion for everything that life has to offer. You can still bring a lot vigor and determination to your world no matter how creaky your knees may be or how many joints have been replaced." For the record, Fonda has had surgeries to replace both knees and hips. Go, Jane, go.

Earlier in the book, I talked about that critical and nasty inner voice that has undermined me my entire life. I promised that when it shouts "Too old!" I'll be sure to reply, in all caps: "SHUT THE F*CK UP!"

Where did I learn language like that? Well, from my parents, of course.

Acknowledgments

Ironically, I'll start by thanking my parents, Margot S. and Richard Petrow, who, had they not gotten older and made more than a few mistakes, would have left me no book to write. To paraphrase Frank Sinatra, they did it their way, which is what their parents did before them, and what I imagine I'll do, too.

I've known Richard Pine, my literary agent, for twenty-five years now. All I can say is this: He's wise and experienced in his professional line of work, and equally so as an uncredentialed counselor or therapist. And I'm grateful for his friendship as we move into the next quarter century together. Many thanks to the rest of the staff at Inkwell Management as well.

I'm also grateful to everyone at Kensington Books, especially my editor, Denise Silvestro, who edits with a light touch but with maximum impact. Also sincere thanks to publisher Lynn Cully, who has been a big supporter of the book, publicist Ann Pryor, cover designer Barbara Brown, production editor Arthur Maisel, and copyeditor Karen Krumpak.

The title essay of this book was originally published in *The New York Times* in a different form but with much the same message (as have a few others). How lucky I am to have had Toby Bilanow as my longtime editor at *The New York Times*, and to have had our professional relationship turn into a friendship. And a special word of thanks to Mike Winerip, the former *Times* reporter and editor who gave me my first big break at the "Gray Lady," and Greg Brock, now retired from the paper, who was my guardian angel.

I've also written extensively for the Health/Science section at the *Washington Post*, notably for editor Margaret "Pooh" Shapiro, whose kindness is matched only by her skilled editing. (Again, some of the chapters here are adapted from my *Post* columns.) Thanks also to her partner in crime, Kathy Lally. And I am eternally appreciative to Lena H. Sun, a *Post* reporter, and more importantly, a friend for four decades.

A few years ago, I wrote a column for *The Times* and quoted the short poem by Mary Oliver called "The Uses of Sorrow," where she wrote about the gifts that came from loss. Over these recent years, I've been lucky to have many friends and colleagues who are gifts, some shiny and new, others worn and still loved. Some read chapters of this book; others listened to me when I needed an ear; all took care of me when I needed that support. Thank you to:

Amy Barr, Bridget Booher, Steven Burke and Randy Campbell, Wendy and Charlie Couch, Bartow Culp, Vince Errico, Charlotte Eyerman, Julie Fenster, Debbie and Arthur Finn, Robert Goldberg and Terri Flam, Amy

Gorely, Debbie Hill and Julia Mack, Eric Marcus, Elizabeth Matheson, Jim May and Rich Cox, Susan Mandell, Jill McCorkle and Tom Rankin, David Payne and Kate Paisley Kennedy, Tori Reynolds and John Beerman, Fred Silverman, Mark and Jennifer Solomon, Phil Spiro, Lee Smith, Peter L. Stein, Cyndi Stivers, Margaret Sullivan, Vicki Threlfall and Molly O'Neill, Tess O'Neill, Judy Twersky and Jennifer Bristol, Daniel and Laura Wallace, Elizabeth Woodman and Eric Hallman, Kari Wilkerson, Doug and Jerry Zinn.

I am also remembering Denise Kessler, Marion Loeb, Laila Mickler, Barry R. Owen, and Jacqueline Zinn.

Ross von Metzke has been my social media director for many years now and how fortunate am I that he often knows what I think even before I do—and that he understands and can explain to me each new iteration of Facebook, Twitter, Instagram, Snap, and whatever else comes along. And that he lives on the West Coast, so it appears to my followers that I am awake 24/7 posting and tweeting. He, too, has long ago become a good and wise friend.

While I take full responsibility for everything in these pages, Roseann Henry is really the organizing force in much of my professional life. On a regular basis, she top edits nearly all of my work—quickly, expertly, and with the precision of a surgeon. As cowriter with me on this book, she was my partner, helping to set and then keep me to deadlines, editing my words with aplomb, and contributing in all ways. I fear the day when her kids graduate from college and she wants to spend more time having fun and less time editing my copy. Her only real deficit: she believes she is funnier than I am, which I must confess is true.

An early draft of this book was written at Ucross, a residency program for visual artists, writers, and composers; I was fortunate enough to have a fellowship that provided me with a room to sleep, a studio to write, and the most delicious "board," not to mention those majestic Utah views, and a wonderful cohort of other writers. Thanks are also due to the Mesa Refuge residency program in Pt. Reyes Station, California, especially Susan Page Tillett.

Much of the manuscript was written at the Virginia Center for the Creative Arts (VCCA), where I've been a Fellow many times over and have benefited from the gift of uninterrupted time. I could not be more grateful to Kevin O'Halloran, Sheila Gulley Pleasants, Dana Jones, Beatrice Booker, Quinn Graeff, Suny Monk, and Carol O'Brien—and to the community of writers, visual artists, and composers that I've come to know and love. For the past three years, I've had the honor to serve on the VCCA Board of Directors.

As I've gotten older, I've learned that there are few things more important than family, and throughout the writing of this book—a span that included the deaths of my parents—I have been continually buoyed by my fellow Petrows, Petrow-Cohens, and the one in-law who refused to take our family name. That would include my sister, Julie, and her wife, Maddy; my brother, Jay, and his wife, Nancy; and my three nieces and a nephew, to whom this book is dedicated.

Onward we go!

—*Steven Petrow*

I am honored to have been a part of this book, and grateful to Steven Petrow for giving me the opportunity to work on it. The book is all his, but it was gratifying to be able to add whatever insight, turn of phrase, or humor (mostly humor) I could.

My own father died too young to have made any of the mistakes described in this book, and my mother spent her older years in the fog of Alzheimer's disease and is thus (mostly) off the hook for hers. I am still, remarkably, able to identify all the things they did wrong as parents, and determined not to repeat their mistakes. I simply make different ones.

Mostly I am thankful for my two amazing children, who give me a reason to grow old, and to my endlessly patient wife, who is surprisingly willing to take that journey with me. After nearly three decades together, Margaret is still able to overlook most of my mistakes, and happy to point out the ones that actually matter. Best of all, we still make each other laugh every day.

—*Roseann Henry*

About the Authors

STEVEN PETROW is an award-winning journalist and columnist for the *Washington Post* and *USA Today*, as well as a regular contributor to *The New York Times*. His essays on aging, health, and civility, often appear on the "Most Read" lists, and you've likely heard him on NPR or one of your favorite—or least favorite—TV networks. His previous books include *Steven Petrow's Complete Gay & Lesbian Manners*, *The Lost Hamptons*, and *When Someone You Know Has AIDS* (3rd edition), among others. His TED Talk "3 Ways to Practice Civility" has garnered nearly two million views, and he is a past president of NLGJA: The Association of LGBTQ journalists. Petrow lives in Hillborough, North Carolina. Visit his website, StevenPetrow.com, follow him on Twitter@stevenpetrow, and find him on Facebook at facebook.com/stevenpetrow.

ROSEANN FOLEY HENRY is a writer whose work has appeared in *Psychology Today* and *This Old House*, among others. She has held senior editorial roles at Hearst and *Everyday Health*, and lives in Bayside, Queens, New York.